주한미군지위협정(SOFA)

군민관계
임시분과위원회 3

주한미군지위협정(SOFA)

군민관계
임시분과위원회 3

한국학중앙연구원

| 머리말

미국은 오래전부터 우리나라 외교에 있어서 가장 긴밀하고 실질적인 우호·협력관계를 맺어온 나라다. 6·25전쟁 정전 협정이 체결된 후 북한의 재침을 막기 위한 대책으로서 1953년 11월 한미 상호방위조약이 체결되었다. 이는 미군이 한국에 주둔하는 법적 근거였고, 그렇게 주둔하게 된 미군의 시설, 구역, 사업, 용역, 출입국, 통관과 관세, 재판권 등 포괄적인 법적 지위를 규정하는 것이 바로 주한미군지위협정(SOFA)이다. 그러나 이와 관련한 협상은 계속된 난항을 겪으며 한미 상호방위조약이 체결로부터 10년이 훌쩍 넘은 1967년이 돼서야 정식 발효에 이를 수 있었다. 그럼에도 당시 미군 범죄에 대한 한국의 재판권은 심한 제약을 받았으며, 1980년대 후반 민주화 운동과 함께 미군 범죄 문제가 사회적 이슈로 떠오르자 협정을 개정해야 한다는 목소리가 커지게 되었다. 이에 1991년 2월 주한미군지위협정 1차 개정이 진행되었고, 이후에도 여러 사건이 발생하며 2001년 4월 2차 개정이 진행되어 현재에 이르고 있다.

본 총서는 외교부에서 작성하여 최근 공개한 주한미군지위협정(SOFA) 관련 자료를 담고 있다. 1953년 한미 상호방위조약 체결 이후부터 1967년 발효가 이뤄지기까지의 자료와 더불어, 이후 한미 합동위원회를 비롯해 민·형사재판권, 시설, 노무, 교통 등 각 분과위원회의 회의록과 운영 자료, 한국인 고용인 문제와 관련한 자료, 기타 관련 분쟁 자료 등을 포함해 총 42권으로 구성되었다. 전체 분량은 약 2만 2천여 쪽에 이른다.

2024년 3월
한국학술정보(주)

| 일러두기

· 본 총서에 실린 자료는 2022년 4월과 2023년 4월에 각각 공개한 외교문서 4,827권, 76만
  여 쪽 가운데 일부를 발췌한 것이다.

· 각 권의 제목과 순서는 공개된 원본을 최대한 반영하였으나, 주제에 따라 일부는 적절히
  변경하였다.

· 원본 자료는 A4 판형에 맞게 축소하거나 원본 비율을 유지한 채 A4 페이지 안에 삽입
  하였다. 또한 현재 시점에선 공개되지 않아 '공란'이란 표기만 있는 페이지 역시 그대로
  실었다.

· 외교부가 공개한 문서 각 권의 첫 페이지에는 '정리 보존 문서 목록'이란 이름으로 기록물
  종류, 일자, 명칭, 간단한 내용 등의 정보가 수록되어 있으며, 이를 기준으로 0001번부터
  번호가 매겨져 있다. 이는 삭제하지 않고 총서에 그대로 수록하였다.

· 보고서 내용에 관한 더 자세한 정보가 필요하다면, 외교부가 온라인상에 제공하는 『대한
  민국 외교사료요약집』 1991년과 1992년 자료를 참조할 수 있다.

| 차례

정 리 보 존 문 서 목 록

기록물종류	일반공문서철	등록번호	511	등록일자	
분류번호	729.419	국가코드		보존기간	영구
명 칭	SOFA 한.미국 합동위원회 군민관계 임시분과위원회, 제6-15차. 1972				
생 산 과	안보담당관실	생산년도	1972-1972	담당그룹	북미국
권 차 명					
내용목차	1. 제6차. 1972.1.24 2. 제7차. 1972.2.18 3. 제8차. 1972.3.20 4. 제9차. 1972.4.21 5. 제10차. 1972.5.26 6. 제11차. 1972.6.30 7. 제12차. 1972.7.31 8. 제13차. 1972.9.1 9. 제14차. 1972.9.29 10. 제15차. 1972.12.8				

결 번

넘버링 오류

분류번호	729. 419 군 1972 제6-15차	등록번호	511	보존기간	영구ㄹ
기능명칭	SOFA 한.미 합동위원회 군민관계 임시 분과위원회, 제6-15차, 1972.				
생 산 과	안보담당관실		생산년도	1972	

주 ;

1. 제6차　　1972. 1. 24
2. 제7차　　1972. 2. 8
3. 제8차　　1972. 3. 20
4. 제9차　　1972. 4. 21
5. 제10차　　1972. 5. 26
6. 제11차　　1972. 6. 30
7. 제12차　　1972. 7. 31
8. 제13차　　1972. 9. 1
9. 제14차　　1972. 9. 29
10. 제15차　　1972. 12. 8

0897

	M/F No.	1593

3

1. 제 6차.

   1972. 1. 24.

4

공 란

공   란

공   란

공   란

공 란

공 란

공 란

공   란

공   란

공 란

공   란

공   란

공 란

공   란

공   란

공   란

공   란

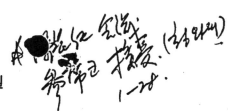

대 통 령 비 서 실

대비정 110-6 (75-0031)   72. 1. 28.
수 신   수신처 참조
제 목   외국군 기지촌 정화 종합대책에 관한 지시 사항

　　　1. 관계부처에서는 기정예산, 예산의 전용 (유용)등으로 마자업에
우선하여 국고 소요액을 전액 지원하고 모든 사업을 최우선적으로 뒷받침할
것. (기획원은 최대한 협조)

　　　2. 내무 (치안국), 법무, 보사부등 관계부처에서는 인력,장비,정보
비등을 최대한 지원 (전체액서 조정) 정화대책에 만전을 기할 것.

　　　3. 내무부에서는 해당 도,시,군의 예산 편성 지침및 예산 책정시
한미 친선을 위한 회의비 등의 현실화 (최대한 계상)토 한미 친선에 실효를
기두도록 할 것.

　　　4. 관계부처에서는 종합대책 (예산,인력,장비지원)을 수립 2월 3
입한 제출할 것. (6하 원칙에 의하여 구체적으로 종합대책을 수립할 것)

　　　　가. 지구별 지원 내역표

지구별	사업별	소 요 재 원					비 고
		계	국비	도비	시군비	자담	

　　　　국비는 해당부처에서 지원하는 금액을 표시하되 도,시,군
비 자담은 변동치 말 것. (비고난에 국비 요구액을 표시하고 국비 지원액중
목간 유용은 유용으로 표시할 것)

22

나. 사업별 지원사업초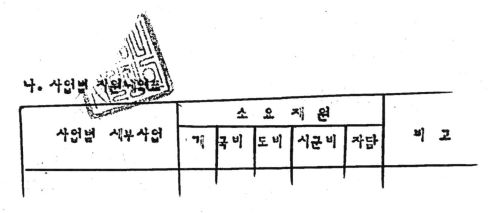

사업별 세부사업	소 요 재 원					비 고
	게	국비	도비	시군비	자담	

다. 사업별 추진계획

대 책 사 업	세부사업	목표량	지구별	담당사업	협조부처

* 모든 자료는 *11* 개 지역별및 기타지역으로 구분하되 반드시 합게난
  설정할 것.

수신처 : 관기부처

디 풍 령 비 서 실

2ㄱ

대 통 령 비 서 실

기 안 용 지

분류기호 문서번호	미이 723 -	(전화번호)	전결규정 조 항 국장 전결사항
처 리 기 간			
시 행 일 자			국 장
보 존 년 한			
보 조 기 관	북미 2과장		협
기 안 책 임 자	권 찬 북미 2과 (72.	3267 1972. 2. 3. 외무부	
경 유 수 신 참 조	대통령 비서실장 내무, 보 사담당 비서관		
제 목	기지촌 정화를 위한 외무부 시행계획		

대 : 대비정 110 - 6

대호로 요청하신 자료를 별첨 송부합니다.

	정서
첨부 : 외무부 시행계획 1 부. 끝.	
	관인
	발송

기지촌 정화를 위한 외무부 시행계획

I. 시행중인 사항

1. <u>성병 관리</u>

가. SOFA 제69차 합동회의 (71. 12. 16.)에서 성병의 원인제거와 기지촌 한국 "크럽" 변소 시설의 위생개선에 대하여 각각 건의서를 채택, 통과시키고, 이를 관계부처가 시행중에 있음.

나. SOFA 제69차회의에서 합의, 채택된 사항 :

(1) (가) 성병예방을 담당하는 한.미 관계당국은 성병 보균자로 하여금 치료토록하고 완치될때까지 공중으로부터 격리 할것.

(나) 한국 관계당국과 미군당국은 성병의 원인제거 및 예방에 관한 교육 계획을 함께세울 것.

(2) 한국 보건당국은 기지촌 한국 "크럽" 소유자에게 다음 과같은 긴급조치를 취하도록 할것.

(가) 변소의 세척물이 적절히 나오도록 함.

(나) 변소에 수건, 종이등을 비치도록 함.

(다) 변기세척, 청소 및 종이나 수건을 제공하는 사람을 배치도록 함.

24

2. **APO 기관 강화**

가. 외무부는 SOFA 합동위 산하 군.민관계 임시분과위원회에 마약
단속을 위한 APO 기관 강화에 대한 과제를 위촉한바있으며,
분과위원회에서 이를 채택하고 합동위원회에서 합의되는 대로 그
시행을 촉구할것임:

과제위촉 내용 : 마약 및 습관성 의약품의 APO 를 통한
반입을 방지하기위하여 현재 10 %로 되어있는
소포검사 제도 와는 관계없이 과학적방법,
경찰견등을 이용하여 한.미 합동으로 적발한다.

나. 뿐만아니라 SOFA 합동위 재무분과위의 활동을 강화하여 APO 를
통한 마약 및 밀수범 단속에 더욱 박차를 가할것임.

3. **PX 유출품 단속 강화**

미군병사의 외출시 휴대 허용품을 제한하도록 하기위한 과제를
합동위 군.민관계 임시분과위원회에 위촉하였음.

과제위촉 내용 : PX 유출품 (세금 면제된체)이 한국경제에
미치는 악영향을 고려하여 미군병사의 외출시
휴대허용품 (예 : 매주 1상자등)을 축소
(minimize), 제한 (restrict)하도록
미측에 촉구한다.

26

4. 한.미 친선협의회 운영 강화

SOFA 합동위 제68차회의 (71. 11. 24.)에서 한.미 양국이 한.미 친선협의회 (The Korean American Friendship Councils) 를 신설할것을 합의하고, 지역문제의 원만한 해결과 상호 우의를 위하여 각지역의 적정한 "레벨" 에서 한.미 친선협의회를 조직할것을 결의, 통과 시킨바 있음.

양국 간의 상위 "레벨" 에서뿐만 아니라, 도, 시 단위의 각 지역 "레벨" 에서 친선협의회가 조직되면 실질적인 성과를 기대할수 있을것임.

5. 미군표 교환소 증설

한.미 군대지위협정 제19조 2항에 의하여 미군은 군표를 관리하기 위하여 대한민국의 상업금융 업체 (Korean Commercial Banking Business)로부터 격리된곳에 군표 교환소를 설치할수 있기되어 있는 바, 외무부는 미 당국에 아래와같이 군표 교환소의 증설과 교환의 편의를 도모케하도록 요청할것임.

가. 군영 문에 교환소를 상설한다.

나. 관광업소 집중지대 인근에 교환소를 상설한다.

6. AFKN-TV   시간 할애

가. 2월 9일 한.미 군대지위협정 발효 제5주년 기념일에 즈음하여 주한 미군의 교육프로로서 SOFA 합동위 양측 대표 (외무부 김동휘

27

구미국장 및 Smith 중장)의 AFKN-TV 줄연과 2월 중순경
군·민관계 임시분과위 양측 위원장 (외무부 김영섭 과장 및 Romanick
대령)의 TV 줄연을 계획하고 있음.

나. 추후의 이용도를 높이기 위하여 외무부는 SOFA 합동위의 의제로
상정하여 필요시에 항시 이용할수 있도록 협의할것임.

28

II. 계획중인 사항

    1. 인권 상담소 설치

    2. 사격장 관리 협조

    3. 한.미 합동 직업훈련

    4. 한.미 합동 의료평가

    5. 주기적인 역학 치료

    6. 군수품의 오물처리

이상의 계획중인 사업을 위해서는,

가. SOFA Channel 을 통하여 미측과 협의하고, 최대의 협조를
    할것이며,

나. 또한 SOFA 합동위를 더욱 강화하여 어려운 문제는 의제로
    채택, 해결할 방침임.

29

DISPOSITION FORM

For use of this form, see AR 340-15; the proponent agency is The Adjutant General's Office.

REFERENCE OR OFFICE SYMBOL	SUBJECT
USFK EJ	Press Release - Base Community Clean-Up Committee

TO Chief of Staff UNC/USFK	FROM ACofS, J5 UNC/USFK	DATE 1 Feb 72	CMT 1 MAJ Petersen/ib/3417

1. Attached is an article from the Korea Herald of 1 February 1972, concerning the ROKG's "Base Community Clean-Up Committee" and its projected activities.

2. On 1 February, the ROK SOFA Secretary indicated that a meeting of the committee will be held on 3 February to review and approve the proposed programs of action, establish project priorities, and a time phasing schedule for implementation of these programs.

3. Additional developments will be forwarded as they occur.

F. M. ROMANICK
Captain, USN
ACofS, J5

1 Incl
as

70

DA FORM 2496
1 FEB 62

REPLACES DD FORM 96, ... SUPPLIES OF ... WILL BE
ISSUED AND USED UNTIL ... UNLESS SOON ... AUSTED.

☆ GPO : 1970 O - ○-410

Traffic Drive On To Uproot Breach Of Irregularities

Seoul police yesterday began a stepped-up campaign against taxi and bus drivers who violate traffic regulations. Bus girls who are unkind to passengers are also subject to penalty.

When drivers violate traffic regulations, the police warned, they will be referred to summary court on the spot.

Overtime stop, overspeeding, and bypassing will also be subject to stern punishment, police said.

Lee Kon-kae, director of the Seoul Metropolitan Police Bureau, said the police campaign will continue until such violations are uprooted.

On Monday, police referred 19 vehicles, including seven buses, to the summary court for breach of traffic regulation, he said.

Boy Hangs Self Like in Cartoon

A primary school child killed himself yesterday while mimicking what he had read from a cartoon.

Pyong-min, 1 son of Chong F Hawangsim-ni, strangled to dea ing himself at a nylon muffle a 1.5-cm shelf p.m. at his ho

Family me Pyong-min oft wished to prac had seen i which depicte gaining life a dead.

There was n home at the incident exce older sister w ing supper.

Institute to Shipbuildir

The cabinet ed yesterday institute that clusively shi nology, a gove man announce

The spoke the Science Ministry is ta establishing

The decis after discuss gular weekly on the rec fishing vesse the East Cc man said.

Panel Formed to Purify U.S. Campside Towns

The government has recently formed a special committee empowered to control blackmarketing of U.S. military goods, illegal dealing of habit-forming drugs and other elements detrimental to the "purification" of U.S. military campside towns, it was learned yesterday at the Defense Ministry.

Ministry officials said the committee named "U.S. Campside Town Purification Committee" is composed of working-level officials of the Health and Social Affairs, Defense, and Home Affairs ministries.

The committee will study and take effective measures to prevent trafficking of U.S. military payment certificates (MPC), racial confrontations outside U.S. military units between colored and white GIs.

In order to prevent venereal diseases from being spread among camp followers, the officials said, the government plans to build more public health centers equipped with modern medical facilities.

The government will also intensify the activities of Korea-U.S. military joint investigation teams in major cities and all areas adjacent to U.S. military units to crack down on elements working against the purification of these towns, the officials said.

City Pledges Security Lead

Seoul Mayor Yang Taek-shik and 20,000 other officials of the Seoul city government yesterday pledged to take a lead in strengthening the Seoul city's security posture.

The pledge was made in a meeting of municipal officials held at the Citizens Hall. It was presided over by Mayor Yang.

During the ceremony, Mayor Yang presented letters of citation to a total of 60 exemplary city and police officials for their contributions to the improvement of city programs last year.

---

tion program, under which 10 domestic business firms will benefit this year.

According to the spokesman, the organization also plans to sponsor a Korea-Japan top-management seminar here in March to discuss the effective ways and means to get over the current business difficulty.

The management consultation project and the seminar are to be conducted in cooperation with the International Management Cooperation Committee (IMCC) in Japan. The committee will dispatch 10 experts for management consultation and three persons for the seminar, he disclosed.

Miss Pang Freed From Detention

Actress Pang Song-ja, 30, was released from police detention after the Seoul District Criminal Court ruled that there is no need to place her under detention it is not feared she would flee or destroy evidence.

The actress was arrested in connection with the shooting and injuring of a burglar by her Air Force boy friend at her home last month.

기 안 용 지

분류기호	미이	(전화번호)	전 결 규 정 조 항	
문서번호			장 관 전 결 사 항	

처리기간				
시행일자				
보존년한		차 관	장 관	

보조기관	차관보			협 조
	구미국장	1/21/28		
	북미2과장			
기안책임자	군 찬 북미2과 (72. 1. 27)			

경유		발		동
수신	품 의			제
참조		신		

제 목	SOFA 합동위 양측 대표의 USFK-TV 출연

1. 2월 9일 한.미 군대지위협정 발효 제5주년 기념일에 즈음하여
   미측은 특히 주한미군에게 SOFA 의 활동사항을 알리기 위한
   교육프로로서 아래사항을 제의하여 왔읍니다.

   가. 한.미 합동위 양측 대표의 합동 TV 출연 (2. 9. 저녁)

   나. 한.미 군민관계 임시분과위원장 (북미 2과장과 Romanick 대령;
       방송일자 미정)

   다. 공동 기자회견

2. 이상의 제의중 기자회견은 특별발표문 (Special Press Release)
   로 대행하고 USFK-TV 출연 요청은 이를 수락코저하오니 재가하여
   주시기 바랍니다. 끝.

공통서식 1-2 (갑)
1967. 4. 4 승인

190mm×268mm 중질지 7 g/m²
조 달 청 1,000,000매 인쇄

Script for SOFA Fifth Anniversary
TV Program

72.2.?

The ninth of February is the fifth anniversary of the effective date of the Republic of Korea-United States Status of Forces Agreement, or as it is commonly referred to--the "SOFA." In commemoration of this occasion, we have with us this evening two gentlemen who are the representatives of their respective governments, responsible for the implementation of the SOFA.

Questions which sometimes arise are what are Status of Forces Agreements and why are they necessary? Basically, the many SOFA agreements which the United States has negotiated with its allies are directly related to mutual defense treaties which the United States has negotiated with many countries including the Republic of Korea. As a part of the US contribution toward the mutual defense of the free world, the United States has stationed US armed forces in various allied countries. The United States and most countries where US troops were stationed have agreed that it is necessary and desirable to negotiate a separate agreement, a so-called "SOFA," establishing and defining the status of the US military and civilian personnel stationed within the host country.

In the Republic of Korea, negotiations for a SOFA began in earnest in 1962 and culminated with the signing of the ROK-US SOFA in the

Capitol Building in Seoul on 9 July 1966.

Picture of Signing - #1

Secretary of State Rusk signed on behalf of the United States and Foreign Minister Lee signed on behalf of the Republic of Korea. Assisting Foreign Minister Lee is the current Republic of Korea Representative, Mr. KIM Dong-Whie (Whie pronoun'd like English "fee") who at that time was Chief of the Treaty Section in the Ministry of Foreign Affairs. Assisting Secretary Rusk is Mr. Robert Kinney, who is currently the US Secretary to the Joint Committee.

Ratification procedures were completed on 9 November 1966, and the SOFA entered into force three months later on 9 February 1967. Article XXVIII of the SOFA provides a ROK-US Joint Committee to be established as a means for consultation between the two Governments in the implementation of the SOFA. The Korean and American Representatives are assisted in the operation of the Joint Committee by deputies and a staff.

#2 Picture of a JC Meeting

Here we see a picture of one of the 70 formal ROK-US Joint Committee meetings which have been held since 1967. Joint Committee meetings are usually held monthly with the US and ROK Representatives alternating as hosts. When the US Representative is host, Lieutenant General Robert N. Smith presides, and the meeting is held in the US SOFA Conference Room in Yongsan.

2

#3 Picture of SOFA Conference Room

Dong-Whie

When the ROK Representative is host, Mr. Kim/presides and the meeting is held in the Ministry of Foreign Affairs Conference Room in the ROK Capitol Building.

#4 Picture of ROK Capitol Building

The detailed and technical work of the Joint Committee is performed by the ROK and US SOFA Secretariats and by twelve subcommittees under the direction of the US and ROK Representatives. These Subcommittees have been assigned over 1200 formal tasks by the Joint Committee in the past five years and the Subcommittees have submitted agreed recom...ndations to the Joint Committee on almost all of these tasks. These recommendations become effective when approved by the ROK and US Representatives.

The most active Subcommittees are those relating to facilities and areas, criminal jurisdiction, finance, labor, commerce, and civil-military relations. This last Subcommittee, the Ad Hoc Subcommittee on Civil-Military Relations, which was established in September 1971, is of special interest to the individual US serviceman because this Subcommittee is working to improve relations between US servicemen and Koreans who live, work, and operate businesses in Korean communities adjacent to US military installations.

3

Introductions

First, I would like to introduce Mr. KIM Dong-Whie, the Republic of Korea Representative to the ROK-US SOFA Joint Committee, who is the Director of the Bureau of European and American Affairs in the Republic of Korea Ministry of Foreign Affairs. It is a pleasure to have you with us tonight, Mr. Kim.

Next, I would like to introduce the United States Representative to the Joint Committee, Lieutenant General Robert N. Smith, who is also the Chief of Staff of United States Forces, Korea. Good evening, General Smith.

Questions by the Moderator

(In directing specific questions to either the US or ROK Representatives, both should be given the opportunity to make any comments they may desire on each question.)

①. Mr. Kim, let me ask you the first question. Since you participated in the negotiation of the SOFA in 1965 and 1966 and you recently returned from a tour of duty in the ROK Embassy in Washington to serve as your Government's Representative on the ROK-US SOFA Joint Committee, what would you say is the most important contribution of the ROK-US SOFA?

4

136.

2. General Smith, I understand that you have served as the US Representative to the Joint Committee for 34 months, more than one half the time that the SOFA has been in force. How would you characterize the effectiveness of the operations and the contributions of the Joint Committee?

3. Mr. Kim, the SOFA provides that the ROK Government may assume criminal jurisdiction over USFK personnel under certain circumstances How has the SOFA Criminal Jurisdiction Article been implemented, from the Korean point of view?

4. General Smith, one of the most important articles in the SOFA is the Labor Article. What has been the experience of the Joint Committee in the implementation of this article?

5. Mr. Kim, since the ROK-US Joint Committee usually meets once a month, how does the Joint Committee have the necessary flexibility to meet urgent situations or take exigent actions?

6. General Smith, I have been informed that a recent example of the flexibility in the operation of the Joint Committee is reflected in the formation and operation of the Ad Hoc Subcommittee on Civil-Military Relations. Would you tell us about this development?

5

(7.) Mr. Kim, I understand that your Government is actively working on civil-military relations through the Ad Hoc Subcommittee and also has recently established a ROK inter-ministerial "Base Community Clean-Up Committee" to work on problems of the Korean communities adjacent to US military installations. Could you tell us your Government's actions in these matters?

(8) General Smith, prior to the SOFA, the USFK had the responsibility for the settlement of claims involving USFK personnel, but this responsibility has been made a ROK Government responsibility under the SOFA. How is the new system working?

(9) Mr. Kim, I understand that you would like to comment on some other aspects of the implementation of the SOFA, such as the provisions on customs and duties, and local law enforcement.

Concluding Questions

10. General Smith, how long does the SOFA remain in force? What do you see in the future for the SOFA and the Joint Committee?

(The SOFA provides that the Agreement will remain in force as long as the 1954 US-ROK Mutual Defense Treaty remains in force, unless terminated by agreement by the two Governments. This will provide a basis for concluding remarks.)

6

11. Mr. Kim, how does your Government view the future of the SOFA and the Joint Committee, after five years of successful implementation of the Agreement?

7

ROK-US Joint Committee Press Release
Fifth Anniversary of Entry into Force of SOFA
9 February 1972

The fifth anniversary of the entry into force of the ROK-US Status

of Forces Agreement (SOFA) is being observed on 9 February 1972.

The ROK-US SOFA is a comprehensive agreement containing 31 arti-

cles covering almost all facets of the relations between the ROK and

US Governments relating to the presence of US military forces in

Korea. The SOFA provides that this agreement will remain in force

while the 1954 ROK-US Defense Treaty remains in force unless term-

inated earlier by agreement between the two Governments.

The successful implementation of the SOFA during its first five

years has been the work of the ROK-US Joint Committee which was

established in accordance with SOFA provisions to implement this

Agreement and to deal with all problems except those concerning tele-

communications. This Government-to-Government body, which in-

cludes a ROK Representative who is the Director of the Bureau of Euro-

pean and American Affairs and a US Representative who is the Chief of

Staff, United States Forces, Korea, has held seventy formal meetings

and innumerable other conferences in the last five years, and has taken

up hundreds of topics relating to the implementation of the ROK-US

SOFA. The current ROK Representative, Mr. KIM Dong-Whie, Direc-

tor of the European and American Bureau of the Foreign Ministry, is

40

assisted on the Joint Committee by eight senior Bureau directors from six major Ministries as well as by a SOFA Secretariat which is headed by the Chief of the North America Second Section of the MOFA, Mr. KIM Young Sup. The US Representative who, for the past 34 months, has been Lieutenant General Robert N. Smith, Chief of Staff, USFK, is supported on the US component of the Joint Committee, by representatives of all the major components of USFK as well as by the USFK Staff Judge Advocate, an Embassy SOFA Political Advisor, and a US SOFA Secretariat which is headed by the senior American civilian officer in USFK, Mr. Robert A. Kinney.

Since the Joint Committee deals with all problems relating to the presence of US forces in the ROK, it has organized 12 joint ROK-US Subcommittees for the purpose of giving advice and making recommendations to the Joint Committee. During the first five years of operations, the Joint Committee has assigned a total of 1212 tasks to these Subcommittees. The Subcommittees have submitted mutually agreed recommendations on 1176 of these tasks, which, in turn, have been approved by the ROK-US Joint Committee. Many of the 36 tasks outstanding at this time were recently assigned to the respective Subcommittees for deliberation and recommendation. The SOFA provides that in the event the Joint Committee cannot resolve a problem, the problem shall be referred to the respective Governments. Thus far, in its

2

first five years of operations, the Joint Committee has not referred any problems to higher levels of their Governments for it has either resolved them on a mutually satisfactory basis, or is still working on them.

One of the busiest of the twelve Joint Committee Subcommittees is its Facilities and Areas Subcommittee, which deals with the acquisition and release of facilities and areas required by the United States military forces in the ROK. During the first five years of the SOFA, the Joint Committee has assigned 1139 tasks to this Subcommittee, and the Subcommittee, in turn, has submitted 1113 recommendations which have been accepted by the Joint Committee. Only 26 tasks are outstanding in this Subcommittee as of the end of the first five years of the SOFA, ten of which were assigned within the past two weeks.

The SOFA provides that the ROK Government may assume criminal jurisdiction over USFK personnel under certain circumstances, in accordance with the provisions of the SOFA Criminal Jurisdiction Article (XXII). From 1967 through 30 January 1972, the ROK Government had assumed jurisdiction over US personnel in 191 cases with 157 convictions and three acquittals thus far. Of the 157 personnel convicted, 114 were fined, 36 had confinement suspended, and seven were sent to the ROK prison at Suwon. At present, only one US citizen who is in Korea under the SOFA is serving his term in a ROK

3

prison. Many of the cases involving US personnel in Korea, over which the US military authorities have jurisdiction in accordance with SOFA provisions, have been tried by US military courts martial. The ROK Government, however, assumes jurisdiction over cases "of particular importance" to the Republic of Korea.

The SOFA Labor Article (XVII) has exerted a positive influence in developing stable and effective labor relations between the USFK and its more than 27,000 Korean direct-hire and US invited contractor employees. Provisions of Article XVII relating to mediation of disputes has provided an effective instrument for resolution of disputes between the Foreign Organizations Employees Union (FOEU) and the USFK. USFK wage levels for its Korean employees are established on the basis of periodic wage surveys in the ROK. The enlightened labor relations policies of the USFK, coupled with close cooperation of the FOEU and the ROK Government have resulted in continuing improvement in the generally favorable labor relations between the Korean nationals working for USFK and the US command in Korea. In the first five years of the SOFA, all labor disputes have been settled in accordance with provisions of the SOFA.

The SOFA has assigned the responsibility for the settlement of most claims involving USFK personnel to the ROK Government, and through 31 January 1972, a total of 3664 claims have been processed

4

under Article XXIII of the SOFA. Of these claims, a total of 2268 have been paid on the agreed basis of 75 percent by the United States and 25 percent by the Republic of Korea. A total of 149 claims out of the 3664 submitted have been disallowed.

In its operation, the Joint Committee has met the changing situations confronting it and it has provided that in urgent situations, exigent action can be taken by the US and ROK Representatives without formally convening a Joint Committee meeting. A recent illustration of the dynamic operation of the Joint Committee is its establishment of an Ad Hoc Subcommittee on Civil-Military Relations in September 1971 in order to deal more effectively with problems in civil-military relations in the Korean communities adjacent to US military installations. This Subcommittee has made information gathering field trips to almost all the major US bases and adjacent Korean communities in Korea, and thus far has submitted a series of 19 recommendations, all of which were approved by the Joint Committee, to improve relations between US military personnel and the Korean people. The US-ROK Ad Hoc Subcommittee has supported the current program of the ROK Government to improve the conditions in these camp communities through the ROK inter-ministerial "Base Community Clean-Up Committee."

The Ad Hoc Subcommittee on Civil-Military Relations has seven panels which work on specific areas of civil-military relations, inclu-

5

c 44

ding local community and governmental relations, ROK police-US military police cooperation and coordination, health and sanitation, narcotics and drug control, larceny and black marketing, race relations and equality of treatment, and people-to-people projects. It is anticipated that the camp communities will be better and more comfortable for all concerned as a result of these activities.

Other Joint Committee subcommittees have been organized to function in various areas of SOFA responsibility, including Criminal Jurisdiction, Civil Jurisdiction, Finance, Commerce, Transportation, Entry and Exit, and Labor, respectively. Only the Joint Committee, however, can make decisions; the Subcommittees only give advice and make reccommendations.

During its first five years of operation, the ROK-US Joint Committee has demonstrated that the ROK-US SOFA is a living and vital agreement which has exerted a positive influence in the promotion of continued ROK-US friendship and strengthening our mutual defense against Communist aggression.

6

45

46

46

2. 제 7차

1972. 2. 18

47

기 안 용 지

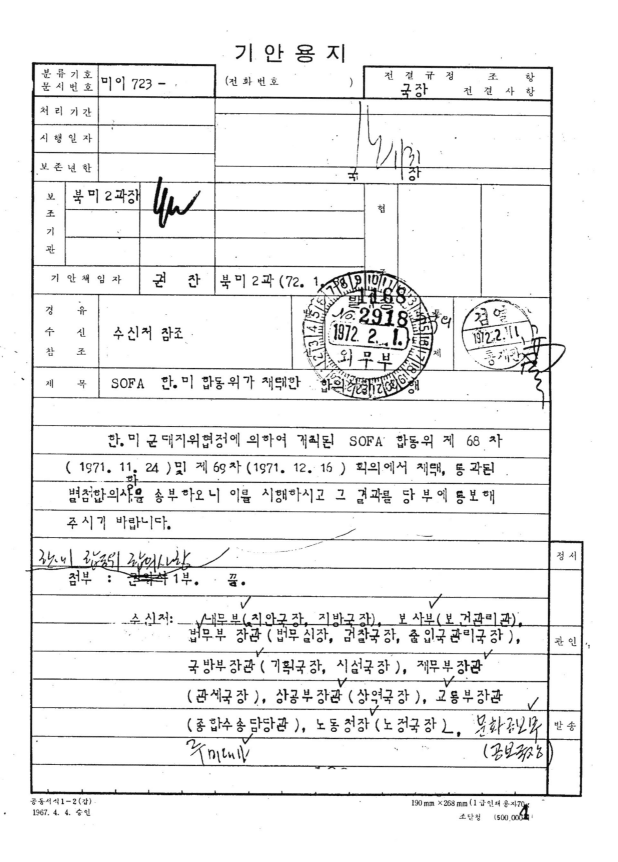

분류기호 문서번호	미이 723 -	(전화번호)	전 결 규 정 조 항 국장 전 결 사 항
처 리 기 간			
시 행 일 자			국 장
보 존 년 한			
보조기관	북미2과장		협
기안책임자	권 찬 북미2과 (72. 1.		
경 유 수 신 참 조	수신처 참조		
제 목	SOFA 한.미 합동위가 채택한 합의		

한. 미 군대지위협정에 의하여 계획된 SOFA 합동위 제 68 차
(1971. 11. 24)및 제 69차 (1971. 12. 16) 회의에서 채택, 통과된
별첨합의사를 송부하오니 이를 시행하시고 그 결과를 당부에 통보해
주시기 바랍니다.

한.미 합동위 합의사항

    첨부 : 합의서 1부. 끝.

정서

    수신처: 내무부(치안국장, 지방국장), 보사부(보건관리관),
    법무부 장관 (법무 실장, 검찰국장, 출입국관리국장),

관인

    국방부장관 (기획국장, 시설국장), 재무부장관
    (관세국장), 상공부장관 (상역국장), 교통부장관
    (종합수송담당관), 노동청장 (노정국장), 문화공보부

발송

    (공보국장)

공동서식 1-2 (갑)
1967. 4. 4. 승인

190 mm ×268 mm (1 급 인쇄 용지 70
조달청 (500,000

48

1. 지방행정관계 (Panel on Local Community and Governmental Relations)

   건의제목 : 지역문제 자문위원회 (The Community Relations Advisory Councils)의 명칭 개정.

   내 용 : (1) 한국정부와 주한미군 당국은 지역문제 자문위원회를 한.미 친선협의회 (The Korean American Friendship Councils)로 명칭을 개정할것.

   (2) 한.미 양측 공히 적정한 "예별" 에서 한.미 친선 협의회를 조직할것.

2. 한국경찰 및 미 헌병간의 협조문제 (Panel on Korean National Police-US Military Police Cooperation and Coordination)

   1) 건의제목 : 한.미 합동 군경 순찰반 설치

   내 용 : 설치 가능한 장소에는 어느지역에나 한.미 합동 군경 순찰반을 설치할것.

   2) 건의제목 : 한.미 합동 군경 순찰반의 협조증진

   내 용 : 한국 경찰 당국 및 주한 미군 헌병사령부는 경찰정보의 교환, 합동 순찰활동의 강화 및 상호 문제점을 토의하기 위하여 정기적인 Channel 을 설치하여 접촉할것.

3. 보건.위생문제 (Panel on Health and Sanitation)

   1) 건의제목 : 성병의 원인 제거

49

내   용 : 성병 예방을 담당하는 한.미 관계 당국은 성병 보유자로
하여금 치료토록하고 완치될때까지 공중으로부터 격리
토록 할것.   한국 관계당국과 미군 당국은 성병의 원인
제거 및 예방에 관한 교육, 계획을 함께 세우도록 할것.

2) 건의제목 : 한국 "그냥" 변소시설의 위생 개선

   내   용 : 한국 보건 당국은 미군 당국의 협조를 얻어 기아 한 한국
"그냥" 소유자에게 다음 과같은 긴급조치를 취하도록 할것.
(1) 변소의 세척물이 적절히 나오도록 함.
(2) 수건, 종이등을 비치토록 함.
(3) 변기세척, 청부, 종이나 수건등을 제공하는 사람을
배치토록 함.

4. 마약문제 (Panel on Narcotics and Drug Control)

   건의제목 : 마약 판매관리에 대한 책임

   내   용 : 한.미 관계당국이 협조하여 공동으로 다음 특정분야에 대한
일차적 책임을 짐.   한국 관계당국은 한국에서 생산되거나
한국에 적법 수입된 마약관리를 책임지며, 미군 당국은
미군에 의한 마약 불법수입 및 미군 상호간 마약판매를 관리
하는 책임을 짐.

5. 도난 및 암시장 문제 (Panel on Larceny and Black Marketing)

   건의제목 : 미 정부 소유차량의 도난 및 면세차량의 불법 처리로 인한
국고 손실 방지책

50

내 용 : (1) 주한미군의 효과적인 작전에 차질을 가져올 정도로
미국 정부 소유차량의 도난이 빈번함에 비추어서
대한민국 정부의 관기기관 및 주한미군의 집행기관이
한.미 상호협력의 기존 절차에 따라서 도난된 미 정부
소유 차량의 소유 및 운용을 검사하도록 할것.

(2) 면세차량의 부정처리가 한국 경제에 악영향을 끼치고
한국의 세관수입에 큰 손실을 가져옴에 비추어 기존
한.미 합동조사 "팀" 의 활동을 더욱 강화하고 증강
할것.

6. 인종차별문제 (Panel on Race Relations and Equality of Treatment)

1) 건의제목 : 미군 기지존 소재 한국 유흥업체에서의 인종 차별 철폐

내 용 : 한국 지방 관기기관은 미군 기지 관기관과 협력하여 한국
유흥 업체에서 인종 차별없이 대우하도록 장려할것. 한국
관기기관은 봉급날 및 주말등 과 과이 다수의 고객이 올 것이
예상되는 시기에는 고객수에 맞맞는 종업원을 배치도록
할것.

2) 건의제목 : 미군 기지존 소재 유흥업체에서 고용하는 접대부에 의한
인종 차별 철폐

내 용 : 한국 지방관기 기관은 미군 기지 대표 자와 협력하여 유흥
업체에서 고용하는 접대부가 고객을 접대함에 있어서
차별대우를 하지않도록 장려할것. 미국 관기당국은 흑인

51

병사들을 접대하는 선의의 접대부를 차별하는 임이 없도록
백인병사들을 가능한 수단을 다하여 교육하고 지도할것.

3) 건의제목 : 기지촌 소재 유흥업체에서 음악곡목 선택에 관한 차별
철폐

내 용 : 한국 지방관직기관은 미군 기지 대표자와 협력하여 유흥
업체의 곡목선택에 있어서 고객들의 기호에따라 균형있게
선택하도록 할것. 한국 관광협회와 미국 관계당국은
협력하여 유흥업체가 광범한 종류의 "레코드"를 갖게하고
출연악사들이 여러종류의 곡목을 연주할 수 있도록 훈련
하도록 할것.

4) 건의제목 : 기지촌 주변에서의 한.미 군경찰간의 협조 증진

내 용 : 기지촌 지역의 한국 경찰과 미 헌병은 한.미 군경찰
당국간의 우호증진을 위해 최선을 다할것.

7. 대민관계 (Panel on People-to-People Projects)

1) 건의제목 : "렛로.고미아" TV "프로그램" 의 촉진

내 용 : 미군의 한국 이해에 도움을 주는 "렛로 고미아" TV
"프로그램"의 중요성을 인식하며 한.미 당국은 필요한
재정적 지원을 우선적으로 하며, 특히 벽지 미군들에게
동 "프보" 를 볼 수 있도록 할것.

2) 건의제목 : 한.미 문화에 대한 가용자의 제작 및 준비

내 용 : 미군이 한국문화를 알고 한국민이 미국문화를 알수 있도록

52

한국정부와 미군 당국은 문화자료 준비를위한 예비조치를
할것. 또 동 자료는 순회하면서 사용할수 있는 "스마이드",
영화 등 소개자료를 포함하여야 하고 한.미 양국민의 지식과
이해를 증진하기위한 한.미 문화의 여러가지 면을 소 개도록
고 안되어야 함.

53

~~한국정부와 미군당국은 문화자료 준비를위한 예비조치를 할것. 또 동 자료는 순회하면서 사용할수 있는 "스라이드", 영화등 소개자료를 포함하여야하고 한미 양국민의 지식과 이해를 증진하기위한 한.미 문화의 여러가지면을 소개 토록 그 안되어야 함.~~

3) 건의제목 : 한국 실업인, 시민 및 사회단체로 하여금 주한미군 부대의 협조 와 지원을 얻어 "가정방문" 과 코리아 헤랄드의 "한국을 이해합시다" 와 같은 프로그램을 더 많이 시행할것을 권장.

   내   용 : "가정방문" 과 코리아 헤랄드의 "한국을 이해합시다" 프로그램이 성공적이고 효과적이기 때문에 한국 내외 한국 실업인, 시민 및 사회단체로 하여금 이러한 프로 그램을 더 자주 행할것을 권장할것. 주한미군부대는 이러한 활동의 기획과 시행에 가능한한 최대의 협조 와 지원을 할것. 왜냐하면 이 프로그램을 통해서 한국의 저명인사를 만나고 한국의 훌륭한 문화유물을 관람하고 또한 산업발전을 관찰할 기획를 갖일수 있으며, 이미 하여 한국, 한국인 및 한국문화에 대한 보다많은 지식과 이해를 얻을수 있기 때문임.

54

법   무   부

송무 723 - 4425   1972. 2. 28

수신 외무부장관

참조 구미국장

제목 SOFA 한미합동 위원회가 채택한 합의사항 시행에 대한 회신

    1. 외무부 미이 723-2918 (72.2.1)에 대한 회신입니다.

    2. 당부에서는 외국군 주둔지역에서 성행하고 있는 환각제 사용 마약밀매행위등 마약사범을 비롯한 각종보건법죄 폭행 상해 협박 공갈 등의 폭력사범및 살인강도 강간등 흉악범·각종군용물 도범등을 철저이 색출 엄단하여 주변의 생활환경을 정화함으로서 외국군인의 생명 신체 재산에 대한 안전보호와 우호적 자세확립을 위한 토대를 이룩하여 외국군인들의 한국에 대한 인식을 새롭게 하고 한국에서의 근무의욕을 북돋우어 국가안보에 기여토록 하라는 요지의 "외국군 주둔지역의 주변정화를 위한 각종 법죄단속계획"을 수립 검찰총장에게 지시 하였음을 통보 합니다. 끝

            법   무   부   장   관

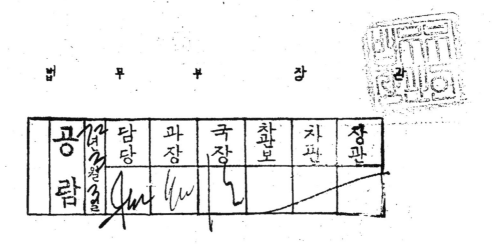

공람	년월일	담당	과장	국장	참관보	차관	장관

55

Back-Alley Club
외란 안경리 내부.

EAKS-CG   7 February 1972

SUBJECT: Continuing Harassment by Korean Officials in Attempts
           to Place Back-Alley Clubs On-Limits

Commanding General
Eighth United States Army
APO 96301

1. Attached herewith is a report on deterioration of the US/ROK relations in the Anjong-Ni Community. I strongly recommend, as a
matter of priority, that this be discussed by the Joint United States
Republic of Korea Status of Forces Agreement (SOFA) Committee on
Community·Relations.

2. This information is in addition to that I forwarded to you
previously (2 February 1972).

1 Incl   JOSEPH W. PEZDIRTZ
   Rpt, frm CO, 23d   Major General, USA
   Support Group, dtd   Commanding
   4 Feb 72

56

공　　　란

공 란

공   란

공　　　　란

공 란

공   란

공 란

공   란

공 란

DEPARTMENT OF THE ARMY
HEADQUARTERS 2D INFANTRY DIVISION
APO SAN FRANCISCO 96224

7 January 1971

Commissioner Min, Chung Kun
Office of the Yangju-Gun
Uijongbu, Korea

Dear Mr. Min:

The illegal activities and lack of progress in achieving required improvements in Tongduchon and the many establishments therein which depend upon the patronage of US soldiers continue to be of great concern.

At the outset, I wish to acknowledge the assistance of Yangju-Gun officials in recent months. In particular, I wish to thank Police Superintendent Ko for his sincere interest and help since his recent arrival in Uijongbu.

In my opinion, however, the police need increased support inasmuch as evidence continues to accumulate that in those areas of Tongduchon patronized by US soldiers, marijuana, barbituate pills, and other dangerous drugs are much too easy to obtain and use. Additionally, black-market activities remain high. Weapons such as switch-blade knives, straight razors and night sticks can be purchased almost at will. Sanitation is poor. Mixed (men and women) latrines are in use. Heat and ventilation in too many clubs are poor. Fire safety conditions are unsatisfactory. Venereal disease is contacted at abnormally high rates. MPC currency is readily accepted. US soldiers are given easy credit. Poor lighting and poor police of alleys and side streets creates an atmosphere conducive to crime and assaults. Too many commercial establishments are in areas difficult to observe and police.

Regretably, two recent attempts by Korean officials to improve conditions have not achieved significant results:

Despite the mass round-up and innoculation of business girls in Kyong-gi Province during 23-24 November 1971, the VD rate in the camp-side villages remains extremely high.

66

Ltr to Commissioner Min

Despite the 10-day closure on 4 December 1971 by Korean officials of two clubs in North Tongduchon (the Hong Kong Club and Blackman's Den) because of "unsanitary conditions", the clubs remain unsatisfactory not only in basic sanitation, but for other reasons as well.

A few days ago, the Hong Kong Club and Blackman's Den, both of which cater exclusively to black US soldiers in the North (black) Tongduchon area, were the subject of a formal complaint to me by a group of black U.S. soldiers. The men specified that the latrines in clubs were filthy and used by both sexes. Heat and service were poor. Girls in the clubs were loosely controlled and more likely to be infected with VD than those in South Tongduchon. They stated that drugs were a menace in North Tongduchon but alleged that they were even more prevalent and easy to obtain in South Tongduchon. These men represent soldiers -- black and white -- who believe that many local businessmen not only encourage black-white separatism, but look down upon black soldiers as trouble makers and want to keep the blacks restricted to sub-standard facilities.

Unfortunately, there remain too many in Tongduchon who encourage and advertise racial separatism and polarization. Only a few meters from the Camp Casey gates, tailor shops, clubs, music shops, and pawn shops display ethnic and racial identifiers. Much of the separatism is at the expense of black US soldiers in the form of substandard commercial facilities and sullied reputation. Much is at the expense of white US soldiers who are not safe in the North Tongduchon area.

Here again, however, I acknowledge progress. Several of the principal clubs in South Tongduchon (where 18 clubs are located in contrast to 2 in North Tongduchon) have in recent months attracted both black and white soldiers.

I am inclosing two documents for your review. One is a listing of minimum standards necessary in Tongduchon for the health, deportment, safety, basic dignity and well-being of all members of the US Armed Forces regardless of race or ethnic origin. The second is a summary of some improper activities observed in the Tongduchon areas frequented by U.S. soldiers.

It is the goal of the 2d Division to establish a joint ROK-US Committee -- at the local level -- which would inspect all commercial establishments in Tongduchon to see if they qualify for U.S. patronage. Those qualifying would be posted with a sign so indicating. Others would be off-limits.

2

Ltr to Commissioner Min

Such a system is now working very well in Paju-Gun. It is hoped that a level of cooperation equal to that which has been achieved in Paju-Gun can be arranged.

In order to qualify for approval for US patronage under the conditions set forth in Inclosure 1, some establishments may have to be relocated or closed. However, Tonduchon does not need an increased number of clubs. It needs to replace or to close some clubs and thus end with fewer and better clubs both on the North and South sides.

The Tongduchon situation must be viewed as a whole. I doubt that the businessmen in North Tongduchon are alone to blame for the sordid conditions which prevail in that area. If improvements in Tongduchon -- both North and South -- are not forthcoming, there is no recourse except to resort to extensive off-limits action.

The 2d Division welcomes your early suggestions.

A copy of this letter is being furnished the Commander-in-Chief, United Nations Command.

Sincerely,

2 Incl   JEFFREY G. SMITH
1. Standards of Fitness   Major General, USA
2. Improper Activities   Commanding

3

STANDARDS NECESSARY FOR THE HEALTH DEPORTMENT, SAFETY, DIGNITY AND WELL - BEING OF MEMBERS OF U. S. ARMED FORCES REGARDLESS OF RACE OR ETHNIC ORIGIN

7 January 1972

a. Commercial establishments (clubs and shops) must be located on roads which permit ready and unobstructed vehicular access to all entrances and exits under severe weather conditions.

b. Access roads, entrances, and exits of establishments must be well-lighted and clearly marked, and safe for normal pedestrian traffic.

c. The streets and areas in which commercial establishments catering to US patronage are located, must be lighted and patrolled by Korean Police to safeguard both Korean and US personnel.

d. Sanitary conditions of the clubs must be adequate to protect the health of US serviceman. Separate and clean latrines for men and women are necessary.

e. A program to effectively reduce the high incidence of VD contacted in the Tongduchon area must be established.

Incl 1

69

f. No food and no ice may be served in clubs. Only paper cups may be used.

g. The sale of drugs and marijuana to US personnel must be stopped. Tolerance of the use of drugs or marijuana in an establishment will be sufficient cause to place the establishment off-limits.

h. Business establishments must control activities on their premises to preclude racial discrimination.

i. Club environment must be safe for patronage by US soldiers, regardless of race. Clubs must be located where they can be observed and policed.

j. Clubs must be adequately heated and ventilated. Illumination inside must be sufficient to identify individual patrons.

k. Action must be taken by all establishments to preclude black-market activity, and the illegal exchange of Military Payment Certificate (MPC) for Won. Acceptance of ration control plates and military identification cards for pawn must be stopped.

l. Credit must not be extended US soldiers.

2

m. Signs on commercial establishments which denote ethnic, racial, or social groupings, and in so doing indicate a catering to exclusive groups, must be removed and/or changed.

n. The sale of weapons such as switch-blade knives, brass knuckles, night sticks, and straight razors must stop. This will require stringent Korean police action as such items are usually kept hidden by shop owners until prospective buyers inquire.

o. The sale of altered U.S. flags must stop (for example, those with peace symbols instead of stars on the blue field). Similarly, the sale of items degrading the dignity of the U.S. flag must stop (for example, bed quilts made of the U.S. flags).

3

January 1972

IMPROPER ACTIVITIES IN THE TONGDUCHON AREA

Marijuana: (Presence of marijuana detected on a recurring basis in the following clubs investigated by the Provost Marshal Investigators).

New York Club
Lucky Club
Oasis Club
Hong Kong Club (North Side)

Montana Club
King Star Club
Blackman's Den (North Side)

Crimes of Violence: (Provost Marshal's office reported the following crimes of violence occurring during the periods indicated:)

	3Nov-3Dec71	4Dec71-2Jan72
Robbery	3	3
Assault	9	14
Aggravated Assault	2	3
Total:	14	20

Venereal Disease: (Number of cases contracted in Tongduchon area based on Division Surgeon's records. U.S. soldiers population in area is approximately 6000).

Nov 71	Dec 71
593	558

Sale of Dangerous Weapons: (Openly sold at the following commercial establishments).

Ro Shop
#1 Shop
Tammy Shop
Gary Store
Kim Shop
Park Shop

Happy Hock Shop
Frankie's Store
Golden Shop
Lucky Store
Pop Record Shop

MPC Currency Acceptance: (Sale of Beverages for MPC).

Liberty Club
Oasis Club
King Star Club
Lucky Club

New York Club
Savoy Club
Rendezvous Club
Starlight Club

Incl 2

Hong Kong Club (North Side) Blackman's Den (North Side
Montana Club   Seoul Club

MPC Currency Exchange for Won: (Following establishments were placed off-limits during the period 1 Nov - 9 Dec 71 for MPC/Won exchange).

Korea Shop
Korea Store
Metro Shop

Poor Sanitation: (Management of the following clubs has been advised of repetitious unsatisfactory sanitary conditions).

Hong Kong Club (North Side)   San Francisco Club
Blackman's Den (North Side)   New Korea
Seoul Hall   Giant Club
King Star Club   Oasis Club
Savoy Club   Montana Club
Rendezvous Club

Mixed Latrine Facilities: (The following clubs do not have separate latrine facilities for men and women).

Hong Kong Club (North Side)   Liberty Club
Blackman's Den (North Side)   King Star Club

Fire and Safety Standards: (Fire and Safety standards are inadequate).

Bravo Hall   San Francisco Club
New Korea   Savoy Club
King Star Club   Oasis Club
Seoul Hall   Hong Kong Club (North Side
Blackman's Den (North Side)   Montana Club

Heat and/or Ventilation: (Heat and/or ventilation are inadequate).

Crown Club - ventilation   Hong Kong Club - ventilation & heat
New York Club - ventilation   Blackman's Den - heat

Racial Discrimination: (Openly catering to blacks only).

Hong Kong Club
Blackman's Den

2

73

<u>Recent incidents in North Tongduchon</u>

The long history of racial exclusiveness, violence and general lawlessness in North TONGDUCHON, and the following recent incidents in the area have prompted this action for the protection of U.S. personnel:

1. 122030 Mar 72: Four white soldiers were intimidated on three separate occasions by a group of Negro soldiers who informed them they were not welcome in the area.

2. 172350 Mar 72 Assault: One Negro soldier assaulted one white soldier for unknown reasons, ripping the white soldier's shirt and then chased victim from area.

3. 202100 Mar 72 - Assault (Aggravated) - Four Negro soldiers assaulted three white soldiers, with boards. A switch blade knife was also seen by one of the victims in the hand of one of the assailants.

4. 202145 Mar 72 - Assault (Aggravated) - Approximately 10 Negroes attacked five white soldiers

74

(including a captain in civilian clothes) with rocks for unknown reasons. One white soldier was knocked unconscious (a SFC).

5.   211700 Mar 72: 25 to 30 Negro soldiers forced 6-8 Caucasians from the North TONGDUCHON area by making threats of violence.

6.   242135 Mar 72 - Assault (Aggravated) - Three Negro Soldiers assaulted one white soldier with closed fists, then fled into North TONGDUCHON.

7.   261330 Mar 72 - Assault: One Negro Soldier accosted one White Soldier for being in North TDC, then struck him with his closed fist, and fled to the New Town Club, formerly known as Hong Kong Club, for aid.

ㄱㅌ

공   란

공 란

공　　　란

공 란

공　　　란

공   란

공   란

공   란

공　　　　란

공 란

공　　란

공   란

공   란

공   란

공   란

공 란

공   란

3.　제 8 차.

　　1972.　3.　20

93

		SECURITY CLASSIFICATION		

SECURITY CLASSIFICATION
UNCLASSIFIED

PAGE	DRAFTER OR RELEASER TIME	PRECEDENCE		MF	CLASS	CIC	FOR MESSAGE CENTER COMMUNICATIONS CENTER ONLY			
		ACT	INFO					DATE – TIME	MONTH	YR
1 OF 3		PP			UU		180750Z			

BOOK
NO

MESSAGE HANDLING INSTRUCTIONS

FROM: COMUSKOREA

TO: CG USAEIGHT
COMNAVFORK
COMAFK

ROK representation is requested at the conference from among members of ROK component, SOFA ad hoc Sub-committee : 2-3

UNCLASSIFIED

USFK EJ

Subj: Civil Affairs Conference, 15 March 1972

Ref: USFK PD 5-3 dtd 13 Jan 72.

1. A one-day tri-service Civil Affairs Conference will be held starting at 0830 hours, 15 March 1972, in Bldg 2370, Yongsan Main Post. Civil affairs officers, or persons in similar positions, down to battalion/ squadron level are invited.

2. Representatives from major subordinate commands of components should attend the conference.

3. Purpose of the conference will be to get the reactions and observations of the local commanders to the recent efforts of the joint US/ROK Ad Hoc Subcommittee on Civil-Military Relations and to ascertain

DISTR:

CmdCtr, SJS, J5, PAJ

COORDINATION: None required

DRAFTER TYPED NAMED, TITLE, OFFICE SYMBOL AND PHONE	SPECIAL INSTRUCTIONS
LTC WALTER KOLDITZ, USA, DepACofS, J5	

R E L E A S E R	TYPED NAME, TITLE, OFFICE SYMBOL AND PHONE	3102
	F. M. ROMANICK, CAPT, USN, ACofS, J5	
	SIGNATURE	6046

SECURITY CLASSIFICATION
UNCLASSIFIED

94
DD FORM 1 JUL 68 173 REPLACES DD FORM 173, 1 NOV 63 AND DD FORM 173-1, 1 NOV 63, WHICH ARE OBSOLETE.
*GPO : 1969 O - 361-084

102 주한미군지위협정(SOFA) 군민관계 임시분과위원회 3

PAGE	DRAFTER OR RELEASER TIME	PRECEDENCE		CLASS	CIC	FOR MESSAGE CENTER COMMUNICATIONS CENTER ONLY
		ACT	INFO			DATE – TIME	MONTH	YR
2 OF 3		PP		UU				

BOOK NO	MESSAGE HANDLING INSTRUCTIONS

FROM:

TO:

the current situation in their areas of responsibility.

4. a. Request the following, or their designated
representatives, be made available to provide short
(10-15 min) informal presentations of recent civil-
military relations experiences:

(1) COL K.I. Gunnarson,CO, 3d Cmbt Spt Gp (Kunsan AB)

(2) COL H.E. Lovelace, Jr.,CO, 51st AB Wing (Osan AB)

(3) COL E.R. Frazier,CO, USAGY (Yongsan)

(4) COL G.D. Tate, Jr.,CO, 4th Msl Cmd (Capt Page)

(5) COL R.L. Marsh,CO, 20th Spt Gp (ASCOM)

(6) COL F.W. Best,CO, 23d Spt GP (Camp Humphreys)

(7) MAJ D.J. Shoemaker,G5, 2d Div (Camp Casey)

b. Presentations will provide basis of discussion related to civil-military relations problems
and solutions.

5. Those individuals desiring billeting will re-

DISTR:

DRAFTER TYPED NAMED, TITLE, OFFICE SYMBOL AND PHONE	SPECIAL INSTRUCTIONS
LTC WALTER KOLDITZ,USA,DepACofS,J5	
R E L E A S E R	TYPED NAME, TITLE, OFFICE SYMBOL AND PHONE 3102	
	F.M.ROMANICK, CAPT, USN, ACofS,J5	
	SIGNATURE 6046	

SECURITY CLASSIFICATION
UNCLASSIFIED

DD FORM 1 JUL 68 173   REPLACES DD FORM 173, 1 NOV 63 AND DD FORM 173-1, 1 NOV 63, WHICH ARE OBSOLETE.   ☆GPO : 1969 O - 361-084

SOFA 한.미국 합동위원회 군민관계 임시분과위원회, 제6-15차. 1972   103

		SECURITY CLASSIFICATION UNCLASSIFIED					

PAGE	DRAFTER OR RELEASER TIME	PRECEDENCE		NF	CLASS	CIC	FOR MESSAGE CENTER COMMUNICATIONS CENTER ONLY			
		ACT	INFO					DATE – TIME	MONTH	YR
3 OF 3		PP			UU					

BOOK NO	MESSAGE HANDLING INSTRUCTIONS

FROM:

TO:

quire orders issued by the particular component.

6. Request that each component provide name, rank and contact telephone number of proposed delegates, and whether billeting is desired, to ACofS, J5, USFK, NLT COB 10 Mar 72.

6543210

0

DISTR:

DRAFTER TYPED NAMED, TITLE, OFFICE SYMBOL AND PHONE	SPECIAL INSTRUCTIONS
LTC WALTER KOLDITZ, USA, DepACofS, J5	

R
E
L
E
A
S
E
R

TYPED NAME, TITLE, OFFICE SYMBOL AND PHONE	3102
F.M.ROMANICK, CAPT, USN, ACofS, J5	
SIGNATURE	6046

SECURITY CLASSIFICATION
UNCLASSIFIED

DD FORM 173
1 JUL 68   REPLACES DD FORM 173, 1 NOV 63 AND DD FORM 173-1, 1 NOV 63, WHICH ARE OBSOLETE.

CIVIL AFFAIRS CONFERENCE

On 15 March 1972, the ACofS, J5 USFK will host a periodic civil affairs conference at the SOFA Conference Room, Yongsan. The conference will be opened by Lt General Robert N. Smith, USAF, Chief of Staff, USFK, and will feature presentations and discussions by component area commanders and the chairmen of the ROK and US Components of the Ad Hoc Subcommittee on Civil-Military Relations, Mr. KIM Young Sup and Captain F. M. Romanick, USN, Assistant Chief of Staff, J5, USFK respectively.

Though several civil affairs conferences have been held in the past, this will be the first since the formation of the ROK-US Ad Hoc Subcommittee on Civil-Military Relations. According to Captain Romanick, this "is part of the continuing joint effort to enhance the relationship between US military installations and adjacent Korean communities. The Joint Ad Hoc Subcommittee reflects the first instance where local problems in civil-military relations have been brought to the attention of leaders at the national level."

97

공   란

공 란

공   란

공 란

기 안 용 지

후결

분류기호 문서번호	미이 723 -	(전화번호)	전결규정 조항
			국 장 전결사항

처리기간		후결	
시행일자			국 장
보존년한			

| 보조
기관 | 과 장 | | | 협 | |
| 기안책임자 | 권 찬   북미 2 과 (72. | | | | |

| 경유
수신
참조 | 수신처 참조 | 통
제 | |

| 제 목 | SOFA 합동위 군민관계 임시분과위 |

3. 17. 15:30 외무부 회의실에서 제 8 차 군민관계 임시
분과위원회 회의를 개최코저 하오니, 각 위원들은 필히 참석하여
주시기 바랍니다. 끝.

| | | 정서 |

수신처 :   내무부 (지방국장, 치안국장), 법무부 (법무실장, 검찰국장,
출입국관리국장),   재무부 (관세국장),   교통부 (종합수송
담당관),   보건사회부 (보건관리관),   문화공보부 (공보국장)
청와대 비서실장 (내무·보사담당 비서관).

| | | 관인 |

| | | 발송 |

공통서식1-2(갑)
1967. 4. 4. 승인

190 mm ×268 mm (1급인쇄용지70g ㎡)
조달청· (500,000매)

102

110   주한미군지위협정(SOFA) 군민관계 임시분과위원회 3

공   란

공   란

공   란

공　　　란

공   란

기 안 용 지

분류기호 문서번호	미이 723 -	(전화번호)	전결규정 조 항	
			국장 전결사항	

처리기간			
시행일자		ㄴㅣ3117장	
보존년한			

보 조 기 관	과 장	4w		협	

기안책임자	권 찬 북미2과 (72. 3. 17)	

경 유		발	발송 85547 1972 3.18 외무부	검열 1972.3.18 통제
수 신	수신처 참조	신		
참 조				

제 목	주한미군의 영외시설 사용

1.   주한미군 사령관은 작년말 대연각 호텔의 화재로 인하여

주한미군이 공식으로 갖는 회의, 교육, 집회, 위원회 회의, 사교모임

등으로 영외시설 (off-post facilities   )을 이용할 경우,

미군들의 안전에 대한 관심을 표명하고,

2.   이러한 화재 참화의 피해를 예방하기 위하여 주한미군이

공식적 모임을 위해 영외시설을 사용할때는 ~~약부~~ 안전 단위부대 지휘관의

허락을 받아야하며, 이를 위하여 단위부대의 지역 ~~공안관~~ 안전관 (the com-

ponent commander's area safety official   )은 주한미군이

사용하게 될 시설이 제반 화재 예방기준 충족 ~~에 도달되었는 가의~~ 여부를

검사 (inspect the premises   )하게 될 것이라 하는 바, 귀부의

업무수행상 필요하다고 판단하여 동 자료를 별첨 송부합니다. 끝.

첨부: 동자료 사본 1부.

수신처 : 내무장관 (치안국장), 교통부장관 (관광국장)

공통서식1-2(갑)
1967. 4. 4. 승인

190 mm ×268 mm (1 급인쇄용지70g /m²)
조난청 (15(00,000매 인쇄)

FROM: COMUS KOREA

TO: CG USA EIGHT/EAGP-SAF/SEOUL KOREA

      US AIR FORCES KOREA/314 AD, OSAN AB

      US NAVAL FORCES, KOREA

UNCLAS

SUBJECT: Use of Off-Post Public Facilities

1. Due to the recent catastrophic Tae Yun Kak Hotel fire, the Commanding General has indicated concern for the safety of USFK personnel when utilizing off-post facilities for officially sponsored gatherings such as conferences, training sessions, committee meetings, social gatherings, and parties.

2. To preclude such incidents involving USFK personnel, it is the policy of this headquarters that component commanders approve any off-post facilities which are used for officially sponsored gatherings. This approval will be based upon the recommendation of the component commander's area safety official who, in coordination with fire, engineering, and medical personnel, will inspect the premises to determine if the premise is safe for use by USFK personnel. Special attention will be given to compliance with fire standards, number of exits, safe construction of building, portable fire equipment available, fire exits, fire alarm equipment installed, and local fire fighting equipment. Requests for permission from hotel or facilities managers or proprietors to conduct inspections of premises should be made as far in advance as possible.

109

3. It is further recommended that unofficial off-post public facilities utilized by groups of over 25 for living quarters or unofficial gatherings consider the advisability of requesting safety advice by qualified safety personnel.

4. This authority for utilization approval of off-post facilities may be delegated no lower than Brigade or Group level of command.

5. This policy will be amplified in the next publication of EA Supplement to AR 385-10.

110

공　　　　란

공   란

공   란

공   란

공 란

공 란

공   란

공   란

공   란

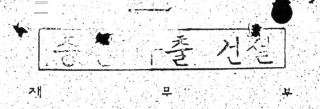

재　　　　무　　　　부

협력 1241.3-232　　　　　　　　　　　　　1972. 3. 4.

수 신　의무부장관

제 목　한.미합동위원회 협의사항

공 람	72년 시행 3월 6일	담당	과장	국장	차관보	차관	장관
		(서명)	(서명)	(서명)			

　1. 미이 723-2918(1972. 2. 1) 및 미이 723-5162(1972. 2. 18)에

대한 회신입니다.

　　2. 주한미군 지위협정 (SOFA) 에 의한 면세 차량의 불법처리

방지및 단속은 부정차량 일소 대책에 따라 계속 실시되고 있으며

　　3. 한미합동 단속반의 활동 증강을 위해

　　　가, 주요 PX 에 세관원 상주를 포함하여 인력및 수시 기동력의

증강을 기하고

　　　나. APO 를 통한 마약및 습관성의 의약품 단속을 위한 검사

강화책을 첨부와 같이 수립 강구하고 있읍니다

첨부 : 1. 관세청 공문사본 1부.

　　　2. 군용품 도난방지및 마약단속 방안 1부

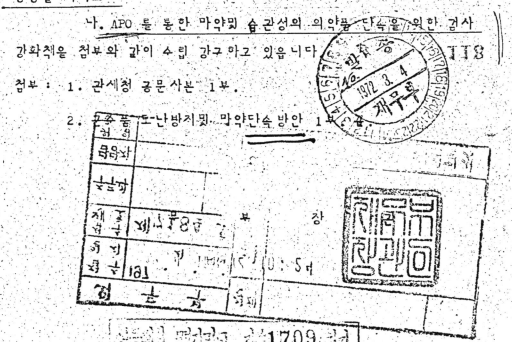

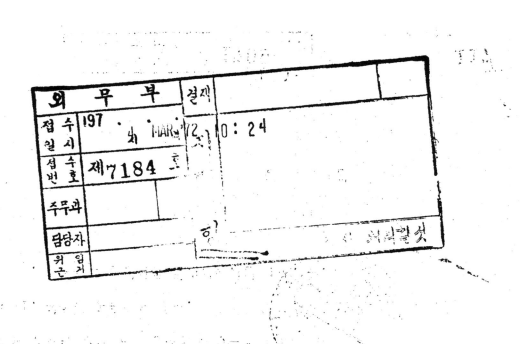

외 무 부 | 결재 |

접수일시	197 · 3 MAR 72 10 : 24
접수번호	제7184 호
주무과	
담당자	
위임군거	

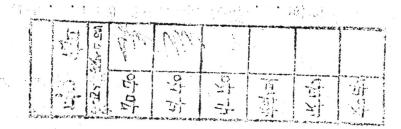

관　　　세　　　청

심리 1245-228   72. 2. 24.

수 신 재무부장관

제목 한, 미 합동위원회 합의사항 시행

　　　1. 협력 723-115호 (72. 2. 2) 및 동 189호 (72. 2. 21)에 대한

것입니다.

　　　2. 한미 행협 (S.O.F.A.)에 의한 면세차량의 불법처리 방지

및 단속은 부정차량 일소 시책으로서 계속 실시하고 있으며

　　　3. 한미 합동 단속반의 활동 증강문제는 외국군 주둔 기지촌

정화 사업 수행을 위하여 심리 1245-151호 (72. 2. 3)로 보고한 바와 같

이 인력및 수사기동력 증강을 대통령 비서실에 요청 (동 대책안 제출)

하였으므로 그 결과에 따라 처리 하겠습니다. 끝.

　　　관　　　세　　　청　　　장

12

事業	細部事業	目標量	地區別	擔當事業	協助部處
軍需品 一般品 및 逃求 防止 (PX 流品 回收 强化)	1. 主要 PX 7個處에 臨時에 監視 部隊 合同 合議에 工程(臨時監視를)	2月~12月	龍山(서울), 高平 東豆川 議政府	程閣處 臨時 回收	外務 部軍 美
	2. 其他 PX 4個處에 巡察 監視		平澤 金山 大邱 堪州 倭館 大德 沐浦		
	3. 申告制 實施 (補償金 支給)		各程團	申告制 實施 (補償金 支給)	
	가. 探報者 補償金 支給				
	나. 探報 장려				
	다. 申告 씨스템(說設) 活用				
	4. 各市場 百貨店 商街 등 巡察 및 流動 回收 强化		軍要 淨化 施設(川)	PX 物品 回收 强化	內 務部
	5. 人力 增員 PX 常駐 및 巡察 要員 增員				鎌
	6. 搜查 기동의 增强 車輛 追 確保 및 整備 개선	3月	高平 平澤 서울	A.P.○ 檢查 强化	保 經部
麻藥 및 習慣性 逃築品 回收	1. 麻藥 使用 常習者 (吸煙注射 등에) 送達 또는 小量의 全量回收 및 搜達 또는 軍美 合同 委員會에 上程	2月			外務部 美軍例
	2. 習記小量로 開課逃築 등에 있다	2月			外 務 部

事業	細部事業	目標量	地區別	擔當事業	協助部處
	同走員들에 工程	4月~9月			美軍시側
	3. 医藥品 分析 鑑定制度 同走員들에 工程	"			保社部, 外務部 美軍側
	4. 痲藥 使用 常習者 通報制度 確立	2月~12月			保社部 美軍側
	위. 痲藥 鑑識用犬 訓練配置 및 同走員들에 工程	2月~12月 2頭	富平 수원 서울	痲藥 鑑識 裝備 維持	外務部 美軍側
		"			
		計 6頭			
	4. 鑑識 專門走員 訓練配置 (增員)	2명 2명 2명	富平 수원 서울	人力 增員	保社部 經濟部

법   무   부

송무 723 5318   1972. 3. 10

수신 외무부장관

참조 구미국장

제목 한미 합동위원회 합의 사항시행에 대한 회신

    제 70 차 한 미 합동 위원회에서 채택한 합의 사항중

당부 소관 사항이 없음을 통보합니다.   끝

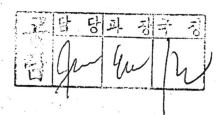

법   무   부   장   관

124.

Mr. Kwon

교　통　부

종수 723 - 332   1972. 3. 13.

수신 외무부장관

제목 SOFA 한미 합동위가 채택한 합의사항 시행.

　　　1. 미이 723 - 5162('72. 2. 18)와 관련됨.

　　　2. SOFA합동위 제70차 회의에서 채택, 통과된 합의사항중 당

부 소관 사항에 대하여는 별첨과 같이 조치하였음을 통보합니다.

　　　첨부 : 한미 합동위 합의사항중 당부 조치사항. 1종부. 끔.

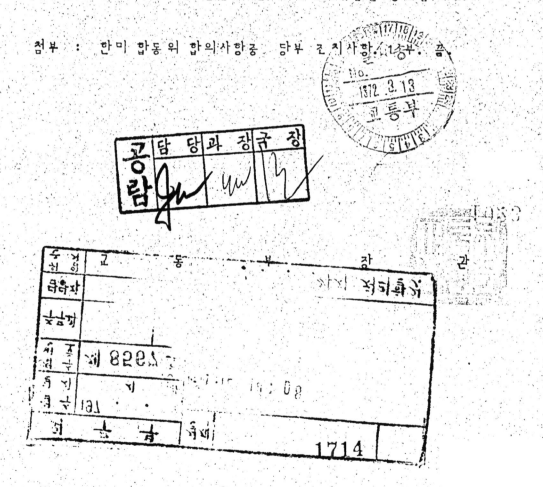

1714

교 통 부

업무 1530   1972.   3.   9

수신 수신처참조

제목 SOFA 한.미 합동위원회의 합의사항 시행 지시

　　　한미군대 지위 협정에 의하여 개최된 합동위원회에서 채택된 합의사항
을 동봉하니 이를 개선토록 산하업체에 지시, 철저히 이행토록함은 물론 지방
유지, 일반시민, 귀도산하 협회등의기구와 협조하여 미군의 가정방문을 장려함
은 물론 도의 주요관광지등에 대한 관광여행을 알선하므로써 한국에 대한 지식
등을 제고할 수 있도록 조치하기 바랍니다.

　　　1. 현지 미군기지 지휘관과 협력, 휴양업체의 상호를 검토 불미한상호
나, 인종차별을 뜻하는 업소명이 있을때에는 이를 변경토록 할 것.

　　　2. 보건위생 검열을 강화함은 물론 음식은 식품위생법에 의한 조건을
구비한 자만이 취급하도록 할 것.

　　　3. 출입구밖에 위생검열 표식을 할 것(위생검열 표식이 없는 업소출입
금지 선포위계).

　　　4. 공무 이외에는 종업원 이외의자의 출입을 금지토록 할 것.

　　　5. 보건증을 소지하고 업체와 관련이있는 여성을 제외하고는 출입을
금지토록 할 것.

　　　6. 미성녀자의 고용 및 업체의 출입을 금지할 것. 끝.

　　　　　　교 　 통 　 부 　 장 　 관

수신처 : 나 - (5, 11).

126

기 안 용 지

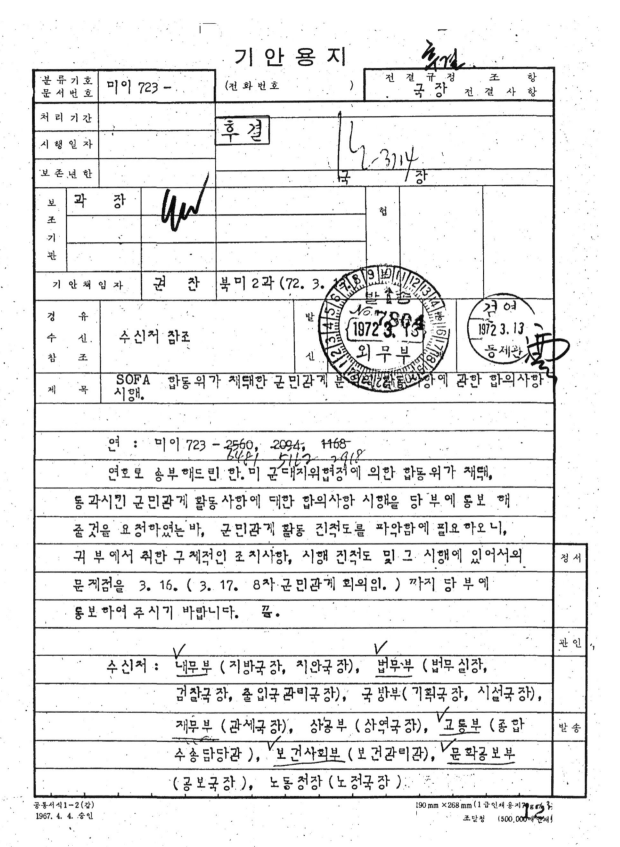

분류기호 문서번호	미이 723 -		(전화번호)		전결규정 조 항	
					국장 전결사항	
처리기간						
시행일자			후결			
보존년한						
보조 기관	과 장				협	
기안책임자	권 찬	북미 2과 (72. 3.				
경 유				발 신		
수 신	수신처 참조					
참 조						
제 목	SOFA 합동위가 채택한 군민관계 분 에 관한 합의사항 시행.					

연 : 미이 723 - 2560, 2094, 1168
8481   5113   2918

연호로 송부해드린 한.미 군대지위협정에 의한 합동위가 채택,

통과시킨 군민관계 활동사항에 대한 합의사항 시행을 당 부에 통보 해

줄 것을 요청하였는 바, 군민관계 활동 진척도를 파악함에 필요하오니,

귀 부에서 취한 구체적인 조치사항, 시행 진척도 및 그 시행에 있어서의

문제점을 3. 16. (3. 17. 8차 군민관계 회의임.) 까지 당 부에

통보하여 주시기 바랍니다. 끝.

수신처 : 내무부 (지방국장, 치안국장), 법무부 (법무 실장,

검찰국장, 출입국관미국장), 국방부 (기획국장, 시설국장),

재무부 (관세국장), 상공부 (상역국장), 고통부 (종합

수송담당관), 보건사회부 (보건관미관), 문학공보부

(공보국장), 노동청장 (노정국장)

정서

관인

발송

교   통   부

종수 723 - *3444*   1972.   3. 16.

수신 외무부장관

제목 SOFA 한미 합동위가 채택한 합의사항 시행.

     1. 미이 723 - 6481('72. 3. 2)과 관련됨.

     2. SOFA한미 합동위가 채택한 합의사항중 당부 소관사항
없음을 동보합니다. 끝.

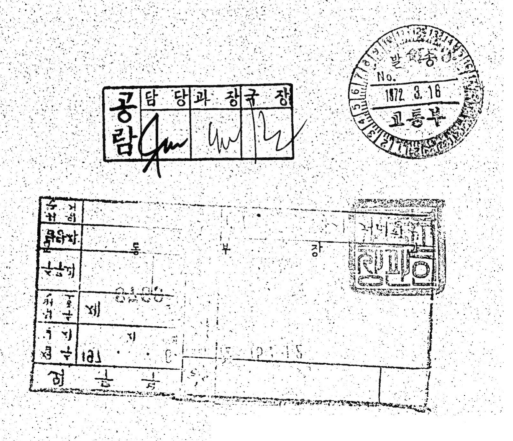

외 무 부		
접수일시	197 . . 16.	12 15 : 12
접수번호	제 8769	
주무과		
담당자		
군		. 처리할것

노   동   청

노사 1453 - 2044   27- 2121   1972. 3. 16

수산 외무부 장관

제목 군민관계 활동 사항보고

1. 미이 72 - 7804 (72.3.13)의 관련임.

2. SOFA 합동 위원회 제71차 회의에서 채택한 군민관계
활동 사항에 관하여 당청으로서는 해당 사항이 없음을 알려드립니다.

- 끝.

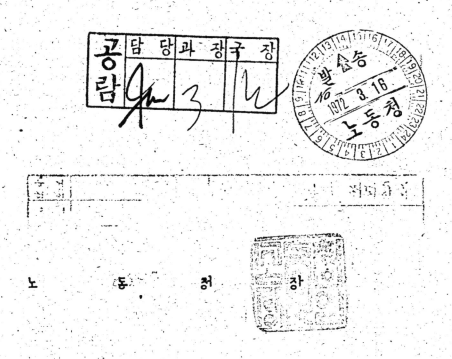

노   동   청   장

129.

외 무 부	결재		
접수 일시	197 . . 16 MAR 72	5 : 12	
접수 번호	제 8765		
주무과			
담당과			
위 근 임서		에 . . 까지 처리할것	

법 무 부

송무 723   5980   1972. 3. 18

수신   외무부 장관

참조   구미국장

제목   한.미 합동위원회에서 채택한 합의사항 시행에 대한 회신

   SOFA 합동위원회 제 71 차 회의에서 채택된 합의사항에
대하여는 당부 해당 사항 없음을 알려 드립니다. 끝

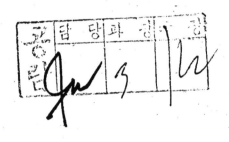

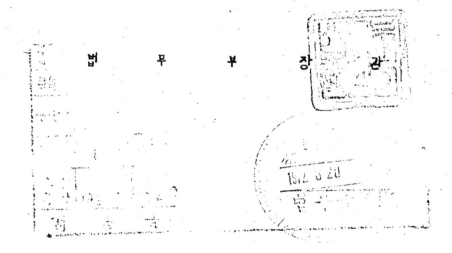

법 무 부 장 관

130

외 무 부				
접수 일시	197 21 MAR 12-13:09			
접수 번호	제 9256			
주무과				
담당자				
위임 국서		197. . 까지 처리할것		

법 무 부

송무 723 5981   1972. 3. 18

수신 외무부 장관

참조 구미국장

제목 SOFA 한.미 합동위에서 채택한 합의사항시행결과 회신

    1. 미이 723 - 7804 (72. 3. 13) 에 대한 회신임

    2. 기히 회신한바있는 송무 723 - 4425 (72. 2. 29) 이외에

당부 해당 사항 없읍니다. 끝

법   무   부

외	무	부		
접수 일시	197 . . 2시 MAR 2	13 : 09		
접수 번호	제 9255			
주무과				
담당자				
위군 임서		197 . . 까지 처리할것		

노   동   청   Kwon

노사 1453.-2/05 (27-2557)   1972. 3. 20.

수신 외무부장관

참조 구미국장

제목 한미 합동 회의 의결사항 결과 보고

　　1. 미이 720 - 7962 (1972. 3. 14)의 관련임.

　　2. 제 71차 한미 합동회의 의결 사항중 당청 해당 사항이
없음을 알려드립니다. 끝.

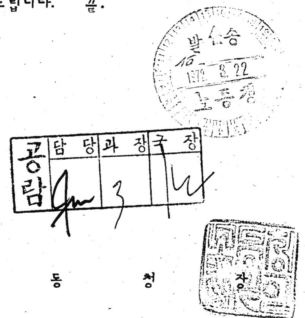

노   동   청

132

외 무 부		
접 수 일 시	197 23 MAR '72 15:02	
접 수 번 호	제 9580	
주무과		
담당자		
위임 군거		처리할것

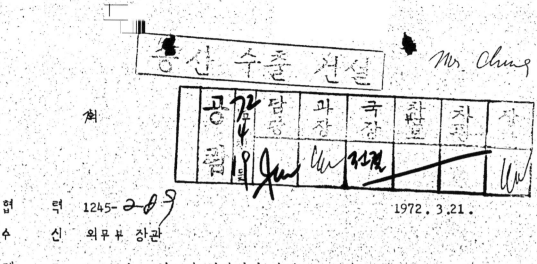

협   력   1245-2♢♢

수   신   외무부 장관

제   목   SOFA 합동위 합의사항 시행

대: 미이 723-6481 (1972. 3. 2)

　　1.　미군 사우 체국을 통한 마약 및 습관성 의약품 부정유입 방지를
위한 세관감사 강화 대책은 협력 1245- 258 (1972. 3. 13) 로 건의한바와 같
으며.

　　2. P. X 및 코미써리의 통제품목으로는 이미 협력 1245- 60(1972. 1.
22) 로 건의한 주류 및 연초와 신규로 커피등을 추가토록 추진할 계획이며 개인
의 합리적 소요량 이상이 판매부정 유출되는것을 방지하기 위해 개인별 구입 가능
한도의 삭감 및 철저준수 촉구 주한 미군 비세출 자금 기관의 판매 상황에 대한 한국
세관원의 조사 및 감사권 확보등을 추진할 계획입니다. 끝

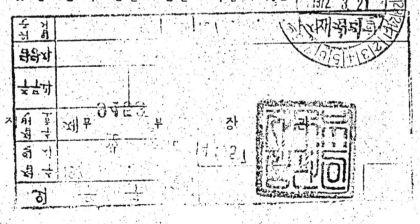

133

교　　동　　부

종수 720- <del>435</del>　　　　　　　　　　　　1972, 3, 30.

수신 외무부장관

제목 한.미 합동위원회 회의결과 시행.

　　　1, 미이 720 - 7962('72, 3, 14)와 관련됨.

　　　2, SOFA 한미 합동위의 결의사항중 당부해당사항

없음을 동보합니다. 끝.

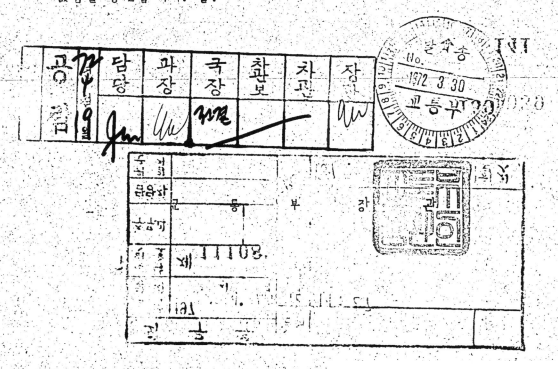

134

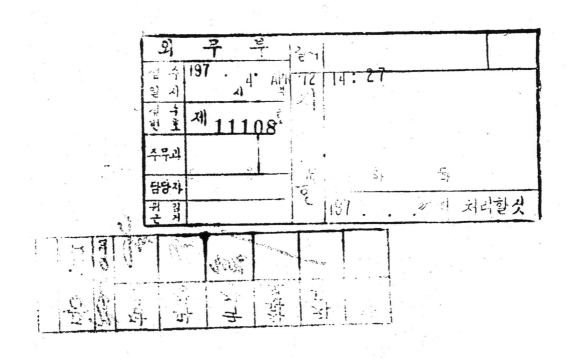

보 건 사 회 부

가족 1434.2-3922   (70-3710)   1972. 3. 24.

수신 외무부장관

제목 SOFA 한,미 합동위가 채택한 합의사항 시행.

　　1. 미이 723-5162호 ('72. 2. 18.)의 관련입니다.

　　2. SOFA 합동위 제70차 회의에서 채택, 통과된 당부처
소관 사항을 별첨 내용과 같이 시행하고 있음을 통보합니다.

　　첨부 : 한,미 합동위 합의사항중 보건사회부 시행사항 1 부. 끝.

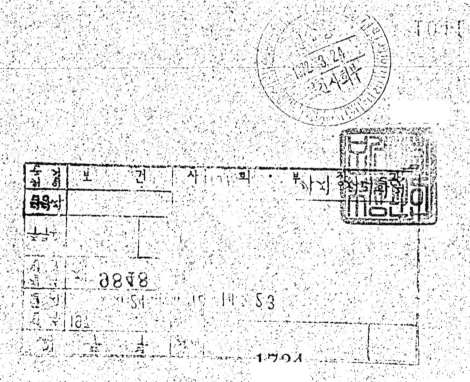

외 무 부	결재		
접수 일시	197 . . . 시 24 MAR '72 14 : 23		
접수 번호	제 9848 호		
주무과			
담당자			
완료		101 . . 까지 처리할것	

보건위생 문제

1. 성병의 원인제거.

    가. 격리치료 : 경기도(동두천, 평택, 부평)에서는 낙검자를 수용 치료하고 있음.

    나. 성병원인 제거 : 년 1회에 걸쳐 역학치료를 기지촌을 중심으로 전 대상자에게 일제히 실시하여 사건 예방에 힘쓰고 있음.

    다. 예방교육 : 경기도에 순회지도반(의사 1명, 검사원 2명)을 두고, 주로 경기도내를 순회하면서, 검사 및 치료 에 때한 감독과 지도 계몽에 힘쓰고 있음.

2. 습관성 의약품 관리.

    가. 한국경찰 및 헌병간의 협조문제 :
    기지촌 정화대책의 일환으로 우범지구에 마약감시요원을 배치 하여, 각지구별 미 C.I.D 와 합동단속과 아울러 해당정보 의 고환을 실시하고 있음.

    나. 마약판매 관리에 대한 책임 :
    한, 미관계 당국이 협조하여 공동으로 책임을 지고있는 바, 한국 에서 생산되거나, 적법수입된 마약의 관리를 책임지고 있으며, 미당국은 미군에 의한 마약 및 습관성 의약품의 불법수입 및 미군 상호간의 마약판매를 관리하도록 협의통보하여 시행되고 있음.

136

다. 미군 병사에게 조제되어 유출되는 습관성 의약품 판매통제 :

현행 습관성 의약품 관리법 제19조 판매제한 등의 규정은 있으나, 동 시행령 제5378호로 명시된 습관성 의약품 및 동 시행규칙 제21조에 규정된 판매허용량의 범위내에서는 처방전 없이도 판매할수 있게되어 있어, 현지로서는 동 법 개정 이전에는 미군 병사들에게 한하여 처방전에 의한 판매 규제가 불가능한 바, 제1차적으로 각 의약업소에서는 어떠한 경우를 막론하고 미군 병사들에게는 처방권 없이는 습관성 의약품을 판매하지 않도록 행정지시를 취함은 물론이러니와 앞으로 한,미간의 기지촌 정화대책의 일환으로 감사업무를 철저히하여 이런 사태가 없도록 노력할 것이며, 계속 한,미간의 우호증진을 위하여 적극 협조할 것임.

3. 위생관계

가. 유흥업소 변소시설의 개선

1) 변소의 세척물이 적절히 배출되도록 시설개수.

2) 화장실에 수건, 화장지 비치.

3) 화장실에 청소, 화장지 또는 수건등을 제공하는 사람비치.

나. 인종 차별 철폐.

1) 접대부에 의한 인종 차별 철폐.

2) 음악 곡목 선택에 관한 차별철폐.

다. 종업원의 위생관리 및 시설기준의 준수철저.

137

공   란

공   란

공 란

공   란

공   란

공   란

공   란

공   란

공   란

공　　　　　란

공   란

공   란

공   란

4. 제 9 차
　　1972. 4. 21

ㄹ늬

이 두 보고서는 4개의 건의가 적시에 시행 ~ 있도록
1972. 4. 11. 합동위원회의 긴급 과제로 이미 승인된바 있으며,
이 4개 건의 내용은 아래와 같읍니다.

첫째, 미군당국은 북 동두천지역에서 맘썽꾸러기 미군을
색출해서 이 지역에서 추방하든가 또는 장기 및 명사조치를
취하도록 최대의 노력을 경주할것.

둘째, 한국 지방경찰 당국은 이 지역에서의 폭력 및 불법적
행위에 대한 책임자를 효과적으로 처도할것.

셋째, 한국 지방관헌 및 미군 지방기지 당국은 이 지역
주민들을 고무시켜 이러한 소란의 요인을 파헤칠수 있는 정보를
제공할수 있도록 할것.

넷째, 미군당국은 미군들의 의한 폭력과 혼란이 남 동두천
지역에 번지지 못하도록 방지함에 있어서 가능한 모든 조치를 취할것.

152

SOFA 한.미국 합동위원회 군민관계 임시분과위원회, 제6-15차. 1972 171

AGENDA ITEM ~~VI~~ V

(US asks ROK to propose)

The Republic of Korea Representative would
like to propose that the Joint Committee approve
the Eighth Report of the Ad Hoc Subcommittee on
Civil-Military Relations, which focused primarily
on American-Korean community relations in the
north portion of Tongduchon in the vicinity of
Camp Casey.

I would also like to propose herewith the
recording in the minutes of this meeting of four
recommendations of the Ad Hoc Subcommittee designed
to improve environmental conditions in North
Tongduchon, which were contained in a special
report of the Ad Hoc Subcommittee on conditions in
the Camp Casey-Tongduchon area.

This special report was approved by the Joint
Committee on an exigent basis on April 11, 1972
to facilitate the timely implementation of the
four recommendations, which provided as follows:

1) US military authorities exert maximum
efforts to identify troublemaking US personnel in

153

North Tongduchon and either remove them from the
area or take disciplinary or punitive actions
against them;

2) local Korean police authorities effectively
apprehend those responsible for violence and illegal
activities in the area;

3) local Korean authorities and local US
military authorities encourage Korean residents
in the area to furnish information identifying
troublemaking elements; and

4) US military authorities take all possible
measures to prevent violence and disorders by its
personnel from spreading to the South Tongduchon
area.

154

청와대 기지촌 정화대책위에 대한 차관 부briefing 자료

1.　SOFA 합동위 군민관계 임시분과위원회 설치목적 및 경위

2.　SOFA 한.미 합동위가 채택한 합의사항 (별첨 1 참조)

3.　청와대 기지촌 정화대책위원회 구성 및 동 대책위를 위한 외무부
　　작업경위

4.　외무부의 기지촌　대책

165

1. SOFA 합동위 군민관계 임시분과위원회 설치목적 및 경위

　　1971. 7. 9. 평택에서 발생한 흑인병사와 현지 주민들간의 충돌
사건은 흑인에 대한 한국인의 인종차별이 원인인듯이 외신에 보도
되어 미국에서 물의를 이르켰고, Dellums   의원을 위시한
일부 흑인의원들은 한국인의 흑인 차별대우를 맹렬히 비난하고 한국에
대한 미국의 원조중단을 주장하기에 이르렀음.

　　외무부는 주미 각 공관에 훈령하여 당해 의원 및 주요 언론 기관을
상대로 실정을 알리고 해명하도록 조치하는 한편, 한.미 합동위원회를
통하여 미측과 대책을 협의하였으며, 문제의 심각성에 비추어 그
근본적 해결을 위하여는 기지주변에서 뿐만 아니라 중앙에서도 한.미
간의 긴밀한 협력이 필요하며, 또한 정부 관계부처의 공동노력이 필수적
임을 판단하고 8. 30. 외무부장관이 국무회의에 한.미 합동위원회
산하에 새로운 분과위원회 구성을 계획하고 있음을 보고하였음. 다음날
8. 31. 주한 미 대사는 외무부장관을 방문하고 "닉슨" 대통령이 국무,
국방 양장관에게 시달한 지시각서와 또 양장관이 미군 주둔 각국에
인종차별을 제거하기 위해 지시한 시달서를 제시하고 우리측의 협조를
요청하였음.

　　외무부장관은 이에 적극 협조할것을 약속하였으며, 한.미 합동
위원회에서 이 문제 해결을 위한 분위를 구성할 예정임을 알리고 미측의
협조도 당부하였음. 그후 9. 2. 한.미 합동위원회는 그의 실무기관
으로서 군민관계 임시분과위원회 (The Ad Hoc Subcommittee
on Civil-Military Relations   )를 긴급 과제로서 설치하였고,
동 분과위원회 산하에 한.미 실무자로 구성되는 7개 조사반을 구성하였음.

156

2. SOFA 한.미 합동위가 채택한 합의사항 (별첨 1 참조)

3. 청와대 기지촌 정화 대책위 구성 및 동 대책위를 위한 외무부 작업 경위

   가. 1971. 12. 청와대에서는 외국 기지촌 주변의 제반 문제점에 대한 획기적인 대책을 강구하기 위하여 청와대 정무수석 비서관을 위원장으로 하고, 관계부처 차관급을 위원으로 하는 "외국군 기지촌 정화대책위원회" 를 구성하였음.

   나. 1971. 12. 27. 청와대 내무.보 사담당 비서관이 제1차 실무자회의를 소집하였는 바, 동 회의에는 북미 2과 김기조 서기관이 참석하여 SOFA 합동위 산하에 설치된 군.민 관계 임시분과위원회의 활동 사항을 보고하였음.

   다. 1971. 12. 31. 청와대에서 아래 문제에 대한 장, 단기 기본 대책을 세워 1. 10. 까지 보고할것을 지시함 (대미정 110 - 115).

      1) 성병예방 및 치료 사업
      2) 마약 및 습관성 의약품 단속
      3) 군수품 도난 및 암거래 방지
      4) 군표의 불법거래

      외무부는 별첨 2와같이 당면 대책을 보고한바 있음 (미이 723 - 1168).

   라. 72. 1. 28. 청와대 내무.보 사담당 비서관이 제2차 실무 자회의 (국장급)를 소집하였는 바, 동 회의에는 김영섭 북미 2과장이 참석하였음.

157

마. 72. 2. 2. 기지촌 정화를 위한 외무부 시행계획을 별첨 2와같이 보고하였음. (미이 723 - 2367)

4. 외무부의 기지촌 대책

"기지촌 정화 대책위원회" 의 사업중 대미 협조를 요하는 사항에 관하여 SOFA Channel 에서 미측 과 협조 함.

158

SOFA 한.미 합동위가 채택한 건의사항 目錄 (69년 末 現在)

1. **지방행정관계 (Panel on Local Community and Governmental Relations)**

   건의제목 : 지역문제 자문위원회 (The Community Relations Advisory Councils)의 명칭 개정

   내 용 : (1) 한국정부와 주한미군 당국은 지역문제 자문위원회를 한.미 친선협의회 (The Korean American Friendship Councils)로 명칭을 개정할것.

   (2) 한.미 양측 공히 적정한 "레벨" 에서 한.미 친선 협의회를 조직할것.

2. **한국경찰 및 미 헌병간의 협조문제 (Panel on Korean National Police-US Military Police Cooperation and Coordination)**

   1) 건의제목 : 한.미 합동 군경 순찰반 설치

      내 용 : 설치 가능한 장소 에는 어느 지역에나 한.미 합동 군경 순찰반을 설치할것.

   2) 건의제목 : 한.미 합동 군경 순찰반의 협조증진

      내 용 : 한국 경찰 당국 및 주한 미군 헌병사령부는 경찰정보의 교환, 합동 순찰활동의 강화 및 상호 문제점을 토의하기 위하여 정기적인 channel 을 설치하여 접촉할것.

3. **보건.위생문제 (Panel on Health and Sanitation)**

   1) 건의제목 : 성병의 원인 제거

159

내 용 : 성병 예방을 담당하는 한.미 관기 당국은 성병 보유자로
하여금 치료토록하고 완치될때까지 공중으로부터 격리
도록 할것. 한국 관기당국과 미군 당국은 성병의 원인
지기 및 예방에 관한 교육, 계획을 함께 세우도록할것.

2) 건의제목 : 한국 "크럽" 변소시설의 위생개선

내 용 : 한국 보건당국은 미군 당국의 협조를 얻어 기다 흔 한국
"크럽" 소유자에게 다음과같은 긴급조치를 취하도록할것.

(1) 변소의 세척물이 적절히 나오도록 함.

(2) 수건, 종이등을 비치토록함.

(3) 변기세척, 청부, 종이나 수건등을 제공하는 사람을
비치도록 함.

4. 마약문제 (Panel on Narcotics and Drug Control)

건의제목 : 마약 판매관미에 대한 책임

내 용 : 한.미 관기당국이 협조하여 공동으로 다음 육점분야에
대한 일차적 책임을 짐. 한국 관기당국은 한국에서
생산되거나 한국에 적법 수입된 마약관미를 책임지며,
미국 당국은 미군에 의한 마약 불법수입 및 미군 상오간
마약판매를 관미하는 책임을 짐.

5. 도난 및 암시장 문제 (Panel on Larceny and Black Marketing)

건의제목 : 미 정부 소유자망의 도난 및 면세차망의 불법처비로
인한 국고손실 방지책

160

내   용 : (1) 주한미군의 효과적인 작전에 차질을 가져옴 정도로
미국정부 소유차량의 도난이 빈번함에 비추어서
대한민국 정부의 관계기관 및 주한미군의 집행기관이
한.미 상호협력의 기존절차에 따라서 도난된 미 정부
소유차량의 소유 및 운용을 검사하도록 할것.

(2) 면세차량의 부정처리가 한국 경제에 악영향을 끼치고
한국의 세관수입에 큰 손실을 가져옴에 비추어 기존
한.미 합동조사 "팀"의 활동을 더욱 강화하고 증강
할것.

6. 인종차별문제 (Panel on Race Relations and Equality of
Treatment   )

1) 건의제목 : 미군 기지촌 소재 한국 유흥업체에서의 인종차별 첩폐

내   용 : 한국 지방 관계기관은 미군 기지 관계관과 협력하여 한국
유흥업체에서 인종차별없이 대우하도록 장려할것. 한국
관계기관은 봉급날 및 주 말등 과값이 다수의 고객이 올것이
예상되는 시기에는 고객수에 알맞는 종업원을 배치도록
할것.

2) 건의제목 : 미군 기지촌 소재 유흥업체에서 고용하는 접대부에 의한
인종차별 첩폐

내   용 : 한국 지방관계 기관은 미군 기지 대표자와 협력하여 유흥
업체에서 고용하는 접대부가 고객을 접대함에 있어서
차별대우를 하지않도록 장려할것. 미국 관계당국은 흑인

161

병사들을 접대하는 선의의 접대부를 차별하는 일이 없도록
백인병사들을 가능한 수단을 다하여 교육하고 지도할것.

3) 건의제목 : 기지촌 소재 유흥업체에서 음악곡목 선택에 관한 차별
철폐

내   용 : 한국 지방관계기관은 미군기지 대표자와 협력하여 유흥
업체의 곡목선택에 있어서 그 개들의 기호에따라 균형있게
선택하도록 할것. 한국 관광협회와 미국 관계당국은
협력하여 유흥업체가 광범한 종류의 "레코드"를 각자하고
출연악사들이 ㅂ 어떤종류의 곡목을 연주할수 있도록
훈련하도록 할것.

4) 건의제목 : 기지촌 주변에서의 한.미 군경간의 협조 증진

내   용 : 기지촌 지역의 한국 경찰과 미 헌병은 한.미 군경찰
당국간의 우호증진을 위해 획선을 다할것.

7. 대민관계 (Panel on People-to-People Projects)

1) 건의제목 : "템포.그미아" TV "프로그램" 의 촉진

내   용 : 미군의 한국 이해에 도움을 주는 "템포.그미아" TV
"프로그램" 의 중요성을 인식하며 한.미 당국은 필요한
재정적 지원을 우선적으로하며, 특히 벽지 미군들에게
동 "프로"를 볼수있도록 할것.

2) 건의제목 : 한.미 문학에 대한 가용자의 제작 및 준비

내   용 : 미군이 한국문학을 알고 한국민이 미국문학을 알수있도록

162

한국정부와 미군당국은 문화자료 준비를위한 예비조치를 할것. 또 동 자료는 순회하면서 사용 할수있는 "스라이드", 영화등 소개자료를 포함하여야하고 한.미 양국민의 지식과 이해를 증진하기위한 한.미 문화의 여러가지면을 소개토록 고안되어야 함.

3) 건의제목 : 한국 실업인, 시민 및 사회단체로 하여금 주한미군 부대의 협조와 지원을 얻어 "가정방문" 과 그 미아 해말드의 "한국을 이해합시다" 와같은 프로그램을 더 많이 시행할것을 권장.

내 용 : "가정방문" 과 그 미아 해말드의 "한국을 이해합시다" 프로그램이 성공적이고 효과적이기 때문에 한국내의 한국 실업인, 시민 및 사회단체로 하여금 이러한 프로 그램을 더 자주 행할것을 권장할것. 주한 미군부대는 이러한 활동의 기획과 시행에 가능한한 최대의 협조와 지원을 할것. 왜냐하면 이 프로그램을 통해서 한국의 저명인사를 만나고 한국의 훌륭한 문화유물을 관람하고 또한 산업발전을 관찰할 기회를 갖을수있으며, 이미 하여 한국, 한국인 및 한국문화에 대한 보다많은 지식과 이해를 얻을수있기 때문임.

163

SOFA 한.미 합동위가 채택한 합의 사항 (기존회의록)

1. 지방 행정관기 : 없음.

2. 한.미 군경 협조문제 : 없음.

3. 보건위생문제 (Panel on Health and Sanitation)

　　1) 건의제목 : 면세 특권없는 한국인의 한국 관광협회소속 유흥
　　　　　　　　　업체 출입

　　　　내　용 : (1) 유흥업체 소유자 및 지배인은 유흥업체내에
　　　　　　　　　　　있는 한국남자가 동 유흥업체와 정당한 관련성을
　　　　　　　　　　　가지고 있느냐를 확인할것.

　　　　　　　　　(2) 유흥업체 소유자 및 지배인은 유흥업체를 무상
　　　　　　　　　　　출입하는 위안부가 동 업체와 정당한 관계를
　　　　　　　　　　　갖고, 또한 필요한 현행 보건증을 소지하고
　　　　　　　　　　　있는 지를 확인할것.

　　　　　　　　　(3) 국적을 불문하고 미성년자는 고용되거나 출입
　　　　　　　　　　　못하도록 감독할것.

　　2) 건의제목 : 유흥구역내의 한국 관광협회 소속이 아닌 음식점의
　　　　　　　　　위생문제

　　　　내　용 : (1) 한국 관광협회소속 유흥업체 소재 구역내에있는
　　　　　　　　　　　음식점 (막걸리집 및 대포집 포함)에 대한
　　　　　　　　　　　보건위생 검열을 강화하고 동 구역내에있는

164

음식 취급자들로 하여금 한국 법령에 의한 기본적
위생요건을 준수토록 할것.

(2) 상기 검역구역을 확장하여 음식점 관리자가 거주
하거나, 대여하였거나, 또는 잠정적으로 타인이
이동 깨되는 주변 주택구역까지 포함케함.

(3) 상기 음식점 출입구에 위생검열 표식을 뚜렷하게
게시하게하고 이러한 검열표식을 게시하지않은
음식점 또는 구역에는 미군 출입 제한구역으로
선포할것임.

4. 마약단속 문제 (Panel on Narcotics and Drug Control)

1) 건의제목 : 교육 계획과 운영방법을 통하여 한.미 군경 합동조사반의
              친선 도모

   내   용 : 친선도모 프로그램은 한.미 군경 합동조사반이 공동
              으로 추진할것.

2) 건의제목 : 마약과 습관성 약품의 불법거매 및 매매행위에 대한
              통제

   내   용 : (1) 미군 우편시설을 통하여 마약 및 부정약품이
                  한국에 불법 반입되는것을 방지하기 위하여 미군
                  당국은 우편경로를 용한 약품의 불법유입을 방지
                  토록 모든노력을 경부할것.

              (2) 마약과 부정약품의 상습 복용자에 대하여 아래와
                  같은 통제를 강구할것 :

165

(가) 미군 당국은 상습 복용자의 신원을 확인
하여 본미치료 및 이들을 우송시킬것.

(나) 한국당국은 마약을 상습 복용하는 위안부
들의 영업행위 금지토록할것.

(3) 마약 거래자와 마약 초기 복용자에 대하여
적절한 행정적 또는 형사적 조치를 취할것.

3) 건의제목 : 주한미군에 대한 약품판매 통지

네   용 : 1970. 11. 3. 공포한 대통령령 제5378호에 포함
되는 약품의 판매는 여하한 경우에도 의사의 처방
없이는 미군에게 판매하지말것.

5. 도난 및 암시장문제 (Panel on Larceny and Black Marketing)

1) 건의제목 : 도난 및 암거래문제 방지책

네   용 : 주한미군 당국은 미군장비를 훔쳐서 한국인에게
판매하는 미군인에 대한 처벌결과를 요약형식으로
한국정부에 통보할것.

2) 건의제목 : 도난 및 암거래문제 방지책

네   용 : 주한미군 당국은 한국관계 당국과 협조하여 P.X.
및 그 미써미(Commissary)의 제한품목을
더욱 추가할것이며, 군인 사병이 필요한 적격량
이상의 물품이 흘러나오지 않도록 감시하는 방지책을
더욱 보강할것.

166

6. 인종 차별문제 (Panel on Race Relations and Equality of Treatment)

건의제목 : 기지내 한국인의 바, 나이트클럽 및 기타 유흥시설의 명칭

내 용 : 대한민국 관계 정부당국은 유흥시설의 명칭이 한국인에게 불쾌하거나 인종 배척 또는 인종차별을 의미할때는 미군기지 사령관과 협조하여 동 클럽의 명칭을 검토할것. 따라서 관계 미군당국은 이러한 유흥시설 명칭의 변경이유와 필요성을 미군인에게 주지시키는 교육을 하도록 노력할것.

7. 대민관계문제 (Panel on People-to-People Projects)

1) 건의제목 : 한국학생과 주한미군과의 우호 친선계획 및 이산지원

내 용 : (1) 한.미 양 당국은 한국학생과 주한미군과의 친선도모를 장려하여 회합 및 여행등에 의한 교육 활동, 합동경기, 오락등 여러가지 프로그램을 시행할것.

(2) 시설 사회단체 및 전문기관으로부터 지원을 최대로 얻기위하여 한국학생과 주한미군의 친선계획에 대한 적절한 홍보활동을 할것.

2) 건의제목 : 국제 친선협회 한국지부 및 한국내의 친선회의 승인과 지원

내 용 : 한국정부와 주한미군 당국은 국제 친선협회 (PTP)

167

한국지부의 설립과 한.미 친선관계를 도모함에 있어
서의 역활을 인정할것.   또한 한국 내의 지반 친선
협의 설립을 장려하고 지원할것.

168

#2

기지촌 정화를 위한 외무부 시행계획 (청와대지시)

I. 시행중인 사항

1. 성병 관리

가. SOFA 제69차 합동회의 (71. 12. 16.)에서 성병의 원인 제거와 기지촌 한국 "크럽" 변소시설의 위생개선에 대하여 각각 건의서를 채택, 통과시키고, 이를 관계부처가 시행중에 있음.

나. SOFA 제69차 회의에서 합의, 채택된 사항 :

(1) (가) 성병예방을 담당하는 한.미 관계당국은 성병 보균자로 하여금 치료토록하고 완치될때까지 공중으로부터 격리말것.

(나) 한국 관계당국과 미군당국은 성병의 원인제거 및 예방에 관한 교육 계획을 함께세울것.

(2) 한국 보건당국은 기지촌 한국 "크럽" 소유자에게 다음과 같은 긴급조치를 취하도록 할것.

(가) 변소의 세척물이 적절히 나오도록 함.

(나) 변소에 수건, 종이등을 비치도록 함.

(다) 변기세척, 청소 및 종이나 수건을 제공하는 사람을 배치도록 함.

169

2. APO 기관 강화

가. 외무부는 SOFA 합동위 산하 군.민관계 임시분과위원회에
마약단속을 위한 APO 기관 강화에 대한 과제를 위촉한바
있으며, 분과위원회에서 이를 채택하고 합동위원회에서
합의되는대로 그 시행을 촉구할것임 ：

과제위촉 내용 ： 마약 및 습관성 의약품의 APO 를 통한
반입을 방지하기 위하여 현재 10 %로 되어
있는 소포검사 제도 와는 관계없이 과학적
방법, 경찰견등을 이용하여 한.미 합동으로
적발한다.

나. 뿐만아니라 SOFA 합동위 재무분과위원회의 활동을 강화하여
APO 를 통한 마약 및 밀수범 단속에 더욱 박차를 가할것임.

3. PX 유출품 단속 강화

미군병사의 외출시 휴대 허용품을 제한하도록 하기위한 과제를
합동위 군.민관계 임시분과위원회에 위촉 하였음.

과제위촉 내용 ： PX 유출품 (세금 면제된채)이 한국경제에
미치는 악영향을 고려하여 미군병사의 외출시
휴대허용품 (예 ： 맥주 1상자등)을 축소
(minimize), 제한 (restrict)
하도록 미측에 촉구한다.

170

4. 한.미 친선협의회 운영 강화

    SOFA 합동위 제68차회의 (71. 11. 24.)에서 한.미
양국이 한.미 친선협의회 (The Korean American Friendship
Councils   )를 신설할것을 합의하고, 지역문제의 원만한
해결과 상호 우의를 위하여 각지역의 적절한 "레벨"에서 한.미
친선협의회를 조직할것을 검의, 동 과시킨바 있음.

    양국간의 상위 "레벨"에서뿐만 아니라, 도, 시 단위의 각지역
"레벨"에서 친선협의회가 조직되면 실질적인 성과를 기대할수
있을 것임.

5. 미군표 고환소 증설

    한.미 군대지위협정 제 19조 2항에 의하여 미군은 군표를 관리
하기 위하여 대한민국의 상업금융업체 (Korean Commercial
Banking Business   )로부어 격리된곳에 군표고환소를 설치
할수 있게되어있는바, 외무부는 미 당국에 아래와같이 군표고환소
의 증설과 고환의 편의를 도모케하도록 요청할것임.

가. 군 영문에 고환소를 상설한다.

나. 관광업소 집중지대 인근에 고환소를 상설한다.

6. AFKN-TV   시간 합애

가. 2월 9일 한.미 군대지위협정 발표 제5주년 기념일에 즈음하여
    주한미군의 고육프로로서 SOFA 합동위 양측 대표 (외무부

합동위 구미국장 및 Smith 중장)의 AFKN-TV 출연과
2월 중순경 군.민관계 임시분과위 양측 위원장 (외무부 김영섭
과장 및 Romanick   대령)의 TV 출연을 계획하고
있음.

나. 추후의 이용도를 높이기 위하여 외무부는 SOFA 합동위의
    의제로 상정하여 필요 시에 항시 이용할수 있도록 협의할것임.

172

II. 기획중인 사항

1. 인권 상담소 설치

2. 사격장 관리 협조

3. 한.미 합동 작업훈련

4. 한.미 합동 의료평가

5. 주기적인 역학 치료

6. ~~군수품의 오용 방지~~

이상의 기획중인 사업을 위해서는,

가. SOFA Channel 을 통하여 미측과 협의하고, 최대의 협조를 요청 할것이며,

나. 또한 SOFA 합동위를 더욱 강화하여 ~~야기~~된 활동 문제는 점 의제로 채택, 해결할 방침임.

143

기 안 용 지

분류기호 문서번호	미이 723 -	(전 화 번 호　　　)	전 결 규 정 조 항 **국 장**　전 결 사 항
처 리 기 간			
시 행 일 자			녀 4118
보 존 년 한			국　장
보 조 기 관	**과　장**　//		협
			조
기 안 책 임 자	**권　찬**　북미 2과 (72. 4. 18)		
경　유		발	
수　신	**수신처 참조**	신	
참　조			

발송 No. 11628 1972 4.18 외무부

1972 4.18

제　목　한.미간 군대지위협정에 의한 한.미 합동위 군민관계 임시분과위 회의 개최.

　　　한.미 합동위 제 9차 군민관계 임시분과위 회의를 아래와 같이

개최고저 하오니 과위원들은 필히 참석하여 주시기 바랍니다.

　　　　　　　　- 아　래 -

　　1. 일　시 : 1972년 4월 21일 (금) 15시 30분

　　2. 장　소 : 미측 SOFA 회의실

　　3. 주요의제 :

　　　가) 동두천 기지촌에 대한 특별 보고서 토의 및 채택.

　　　나) Camp Humphreys (평택 안정리)에 대한 중간보고서.

　　　다) 왜관 및 전주지역 기지촌 답사문제 토의. 끝.

　수신처 : 　내무부장관 (지방국장, 치안국장)

　　　　　　법무부장관 (출입국관리국장, 법무실장, 검찰국장)

　　　　　　교통부장관 (관광진흥국장)

보건사회부장관 (보건관리관)
문화공보부장관 (해외공보관)
청와대 비서실장 (내무.보사담당 비서관)

TENTATIVE

AGENDA OF NINTH MEETING
AD HOC SUBCOMMITTEE ON CIVIL-MILITARY RELATIONS
1530 HOURS, 21 APRIL 1972, US SOFA CONFERENCE ROOM

I. Introduction of New Ad Hoc Subcommittee Members- US and ROK Presentations.

II. Discussion of the Special Report of the Ad Hoc Subcommittee to the Joint Committee on the Visit of the Subcommittee to North Tongduchon, approved by the Joint Committee on 11 April - US and ROK Presentations.

III. Progress Report on Camp Humphreys-Anjong-ni - ROK and US Presentations.

IV. Proposed Subcommittee Visits - US and ROK Presentations.

Camp Carroll-Waegwan - 10 May   2 ~ ~
Camp Page-Chunchon - 18 May   7 5 ~

V. Consideration of the Eighth Report of the Ad Hoc Subcommittee to the Joint Committee - ROK and US Presentations.

VI. Proposed time for the Tenth Ad Hoc Subcommittee Meeting, 1530 Hours, Friday, 26 May 1972, in the ROK Capitol Building.

VII. Adjourn.

Col : Colditz

116

공   란

공   란

공   란

공   란

공   란

공		란

공   란

공   란

공   란

공 란

공 란

공   란

공 란

주한미군지위협정(SOFA) 군민관계 임시분과위원회 3

공   란

공   란

공   란

공   란

공　　　란

공 란

공   란

공   란

공 란

공   란

공   란

공 란

공   란

공   란

공   란

공　　　　　　란

공 란

공   란

공 란

공 란

공 란

6. 제 11 차

1972. 6. 30

리

기 안 용 지

분류기호 문서번호	미이 723 -	(전화번호)	전결규정 **9** 조 **3** 항 **국장** 전 결 사 항
처리기간			
시행일자			
보존년한		국 장	

보 조 기 관	과 장		협
			조
기안책임자	권 찬 북미2과 (72. 6. 21)	
경유 수신 참조	수신처 참조	
제 목	SOFA 합동위 제11차 군민관계 분과위 회의 개최 및 제10차 회의록 송부	

1. SOFA 합동위 제11차 군민관계 임시분과위원회 회의를 6. 30.
   (금) 15:00시 미국측 SOFA 회의실에서 개최코저 하오니,
   각 위원들은 필히 참석하시기 바라며,

2. 각 위원들은 동 분과위 7개 조사반에서 제출한 건의를 합동위가
   채택 합의하여 각 관계부처에 그 시행을 위촉한 건의사항의
   집행에 관한 중간 보고 (A Progress Report)를
   청취, 분석코저 하오니, 그에 관련된 자료를 준비하여 주시기
   바랍니다.

3. 제10차 군민관계 분과위 회의록을 송부하오니, 업무에 참고하시기
   바랍니다.
   수신처 : 내무부장관 (지방국장, 치안국장)
   법무부장관, 보사부장관, 문공부장관,
   교통부장관, 청와대 정무수석비서관 (내무 보사담당
   비서관)

		정서
		관인
		발송

공동서식 1-2 (갑)   190 mm ×268 mm (1급인쇄용지 70g)
1967. 4. 4. 승인   조달청 (300,000매 1차)

212

BRIEFING ON ROK-US CIVIL-MILITARY RELATIONS

(Given to Mr. Smothers, DOD-EO) (21 Jun 72)

1. DURING THE SPRING AND SUMMER OF 1971, THERE WAS A STEADY
INCREASE IN INCIDENTS INVOLVING US PERSONNEL AND KOREANS.
VARIOUS FACTORS CONTRIBUTED TO THE GROWING SERIOUSNESS OF THIS
SITUATION. THE DRAWDOWN OF US FORCES INTRODUCED NEW ELEMENTS OF
TENSION INTO TRADITIONALLY FRIENDLY RELATIONSHIPS. ACOOMPANYING
BASE CLOSURES AND RESTATIONING OF US FORCES RESULTED IN WIDESPREAD
DISLOCATIONS AMONG KOREANS LIVING IN VILLAGES ADJACENT TO US BASES,

(SLIDES OF CLOSED BASE AND DESERTED CAMP VILLAGE)

(#1 and #2)

AND RESULTED IN INCREASED COMPETITION AMONG BAR OWNERS, "BUSINESS
GIRLS", AND MERCHANTS. THIS SITUATION HAS BEEN AGGREVATED BY
GROWING RACIAL OVERTONES, WHICH INVOLVE NOT ONLY AMERICAN
SERVICEMEN, BUT ALSO KOREANS AND BLACK AMERICAN SERVICEMEN.
ALSO, DEVISIVE CONTROVERSIES UNLEASHED IN THE US OVER VIETNAM
WAR POLICIES,

(SLIDE OF US SERVICEMEN DEMONSTRATING AGAINST VIETNAM

WAR INDOWNTOWN SEOUL)   (#3)

213

COUPLED WITH GROWING GENERAL PERMISSIVENESS IN THE US HAVE

INFLUENCED ATTITUDES OF US SERVICEMEN IN KOREA. THESE FACTORS,

ALONG WITH THE USE OF DRUGS BY US SERVICEMEN IN KOREA, HAVE ALL

CONTRIBUTED TO AN INCREASE IN TENSIONS BETWEEN AMERICANS AND KOREANS.

TODAY, WITH GROWING ECONOMIC MODERNIZATION AND PROSPERITY, THE

KOREANS ARE EXHIBITING INCREASED NATIONAL PRIDE AND SELF-CONFIDENCE,

ALONG WITH GREATER SENSITIVITY TO REAL OR ALLEGED EXCESSES OR

IMPROPRIETIES BY US PERSONNEL.

2. THE SITUATION HEIGHTENED ON 9 JULY 1971, WHEN BLACK SERVICEMEN

RIOTED AGAINST ALLEGED DISCRIMINATORY PRACTICES OF BAR OWNERS AND

"BUSINESS GIRLS" AGAINST AMERICAN NEGROES IN ANJONG-NI, A VILLAGE

OF ABOUT 6,000

    (SLIDE OF DAMAGE TO KOREAN BARS) (#4)

POPULATION, ADJACENT TO CAMP HUMPHREYS. THIS RIOT AND SUBSEQUENT

DEMONSTRATIONS BY LOCAL NATIONALS AT THE FRONT GATE RESULTED IN

INTERNATIONAL PRESS COVERAGE

    (SLIDES OF KOREAN DEMONSTRATIONS) (#5, #6 and #7)

AND FOCUSED HIGH LEVEL KOREAN AND AMERICAN GOVERNMENT ATTENTION

ON THE PROBLEM.

3. IN REVIEWING THE HAPPENINGS, IT WAS DETERMINED THAT THE

SOLUTIONS WOULD REQUIRE NOT ONLY US COMMAND ACTION, BUT THE

WILLING ASSISTANCE OF KOREAN GOVERNMENT OFFICIALS ON BOTH THE

NATIONAL AND LOCAL LEVELS. IT WAS FURTHER DECIDED THAT THE BEST

VEHICLE FOR OBTAINING FULL ROK COOPERATION WAS THROUGH THE VEHICLE

OF THE US-ROK SOFA WHICH HAD NEARLY FIVE YEARS OF EFFECTIVE

SERVICE TO BOTH GOVERNMENTS.

214   2

(SLIDE OF JOINT COMMITTEE #8)

IN SEPTEMBER 1971, THE SOFA JOINT COMMITTEE AGREED THAT BOTH
GOVERNMENTS WOULD TAKE EFFECTIVE MEASURES TO FORESTALL REOCCURRENCE
OF SUCH INCIDENTS AS ANJONG-NI.   THE JOINT COMMITTEE ESTABLISHED
AN AD HOC SUBCOMMITTEE ON CIVIL-MILITARY RELATIONS TO RESOLVE
COMMUNITY RELATIONS PROBLEMS ON A GOVERNMENT-TO-GOVERNMENT BASIS.

(VU-GRAPHS OF SUBCOMMITTEE VISITS #1 thru #6)

THIS SUBCOMMITTEE HAS THUS FAR CONDUCTED 16 FIELD TRIPS TO US
MILITARY BASES AND THE ADJACENT KOREAN COMMUNITIES.   DURING EACH
TRIP, DISCUSSIONS WERE HELD WITH THE LOCAL ROK OFFICIALS AND THE
BUSINESSMEN CONCERNED AND THE US COMMANDER AND HIS STAFF.   THEN
THE SUBCOMMITTEE TOURED THE NEARBY ENTERTAINMENT AREAS.   EACH
VISIT WAS HIGHLIGHTED BY FRANK EXCHANGE ON MUTUAL PROBLEMS.

(SLIDES OFF)

THE SUBCOMMITTEE, IN ITS FIRST REPORT, PROPOSED THE ESTABLISHMENT
OF SEVEN SEPARATE PANELS OR WORKING GROUPS, DESIGNED TO FOCUS ON
INDIVIDUAL FACETS OF THE OVERALL CIVIL-MILITARY RELATIONS PROBLEM.
THE SOFA JOINT COMMITTEE ACCEPTED THIS REPORT OF ITS AD HOC
SUBCOMMITTEE AND THE FOLLOWING SEVEN PANELS HAVE BEEN ESTABLISHED
TO WORK ON THE AREAS SHOWN ON THIS SLIDE:

(VU-GRAPH SLIDE ON)   (#7)

(PAUSE FOR READING)

(SLIDE OFF)

4.   SINCE FORMATION, ALL PANELS HAVE HELD SEVERAL MEETINGS AND
HAVE MADE 34 RECOMMENDATIONS THAT HAVE BEEN FORWARDED TO THE
SUBCOMMITTEE ON CIVIL-MILITARY RELATIONS FOR ACTION ON THE
GOVERNMENT-TO-GOVERNMENT LEVEL.   OF PARTICULAR INTEREST ARE THE

3

FIVE RECOMMENDATIONS ON RACE RELATIONS AND EQUALITY OF TREATMENT.

(VU-GRAPH) (#8)

IN THIS AREA, RECOMMENDATIONS WERE MADE AND APPROVED BY THE SOFA JOINT COMMITTEE TO END DISCRIMINATION BY MANAGEMENT, BY ENTERTAINERS, THROUGH MUSIC OR BY THE USE OF ESTABLISHMENT NAMES. FURTHER, THE USE OF JOINT US-ROK PATROLS WAS RECOMMENDED TO REDUCE MISUNDER-STANDINGS WHEN PATROLLING PUBLIC PLACES. THESE ACTIONS BIND BOTH THE ROKG AND USFK TO TAKE BROAD ACTIONS THROUGHOUT THE REPUBLIC.

(VU-GRAPH OFF)

5. THE AD HOC SUBCOMMITTEE HAS FOCUSED ON SPECIFIC LOCATIONS AS WELL. TWO ACTIONS ARE PARTICULARLY NOTEWORTHY. FOLLOWING THE DISTURBANCES IN THE CAMP HUMPHREYS-ANJONG-NI AREA, WHICH I DESCRIBED EARLIER, MANY NEARBY ESTABLISHMENTS WERE PLACED OFF-LIMITS TO USFK PERSONNEL AND REMAINED SO UNTIL APRIL 1972 WHEN THE SUBCOMMITTEE VISITED ANJONG-NI. THEN, WORKING WITH LOCAL ROKG AUTHORITIES AND BUSINESSMEN AND THE US COMMANDERS CONCERNED, THE SUBCOMMITTEE DEVELOPED A PLAN OF ACTION IN WHICH ESTABLISHMENTS WERE RELOCATED TO MORE ACCESSIBLE AREAS, ALLEYS WERE WIDENED TO STREETS, AND MANAGEMENT PRACTICES WERE CHANGED TO PRECLUDE THE CONTINUATION OF THE SITUATION THAT EXISTED IN 1971. I AM PLEASED TO REPORT THAT MOST OF THE ACTIONS HAVE BEEN COMPLETED AND THE OFF-LIMITS RESTRICTIONS ARE RAPIDLY BEING LIFTED. THE MOST SIGNIFICANT CHANGE IS THE CHANGE OF ATTITUDES FROM CONFRONTATION TO WILLING COOPERATION.

4

216

6. IN MAY, THE SUBCOMMITTEE WENT TO THE CAMP CASEY-TONGDUCHON AREA TO WORK WITH 2D INFANTRY DIVISION AUTHORITIES, LOCAL ROKG OFFICIALS, AND OWNERS OF US-PATRONIZED ESTABLISHMENTS CONCERNING NINE BUSINESSES IN NORTH TONGDUCHON, WHICH WAS A RACIALLY EXCLUSIVE AREA. AFTER DISCUSSIONS, IT WAS DETERMINED THAT THE OPTIMUM COURSE WAS RELOCATION TO OTHER AREAS WHERE AVAILABLE POLICING AND LIGHTING WERE BETTER. EIGHT OF THE BUSINESSES RELOCATED AND THE NINTH APPARENTLY WILL NOT REOPEN.

7. THESE LAST TWO ACTIONS SHOW NATIONAL LEVEL ACTION CAN BE UTILIZED TO EFFECT BETTER COMMUNICATIONS AND SOLUTIONS TO LOCAL PROBLEMS. THE AD HOC SUBCOMMITTEE IS PREPARED TO JOINTLY MEET ANY SITUATION AND IS DETERMINED TO DEVELOP VIABLE SOLUTIONS DEALING WITH PROBLEMS THAT EXIST AT ANY USFK INSTALLATION AND ADJACENT KOREAN COMMUNITY.

8. USFK, IN SUPPORTING THE WORK OF AD HOC SUBCOMMITTEE, REVISED IT'S POLICY IN THE AREA OF CIVIL-MILITARY RELATIONS. ONE SUCH REVISION PERTAINS TO PLACING KOREAN ESTABLISHMENTS OFF-LIMITS TO USFK PERSONNEL. THE NEW POLICY DIRECTIVE REQUIRES LOCAL COMMANDERS TO FORMALLY NOTIFY AND TO SEEK ASSISTANCE FROM ESTABLISHMENT OWNERS AND LOCAL GOVERNMENT OFFICIALS IN CORRECTING UNSATISFACTORY CONDITIONS. WHEN THE PROBLEMS CANNOT BE RESOLVED.

5

AT THE LOCAL LEVEL, THIS HEADQUARTERS GOES TO ROK NATIONAL
GOVERNMENT FOR ASSISTANCE.   THIS SYSTEM HAS FUNCTIONED EFFECTIVELY
IN EVERY CASE, SUCH AS NORTH TONGDUCHON, WHEN IT HAS BEEN UTILIZED.
IN EFFECT, EACH US COMMANDER NOW HAS A CHANNEL TO THE CENTRAL
ROKG WHEN REQUIRED.   THE NEW POLICY ALSO ALLOWS FOR EMERGENCY
OFF-LIMITS IN SUCH SITUATIONS AS RIOT OR HEALTH HAZARD.
FINALLY, IT SETS MINIMUM STANDARDS FOR ESTABLISHMENTS
PATRONIZED BY USFK.   IN SUMMARY, THESE PROCEDURES HAVE OPENED
COMMUNICATIONS BETWEEN US INSTALLATIONS AND ADJACENT KOREAN
COMMUNITIES AND FOCUSED CENTRAL ROKG AND USFK ATTENTION ON
EFFECTING SOLUTIONS TO MUTUAL PROBLEMS.

9.   ON A UNILATERAL SCALE, THE ROKG IS TAKING ACTIONS TO IMPROVE
THE CONDITIONS OF CAMP COMMUNITIES.   MR. KIM YOUNG SUP WILL
EXPLAIN THE ROKG'S BASE COMMUNITY CLEAN-UP PROGRAM.

MR. KIM

6

EAIDC5   26 June 1972

SUBJECT: Korean/American Friendship (KAFC) Meeting

Commanding General
Headquarters I Corps (ROK/US) Group
ATTN: EACICA
AFO 96358

1. References:

    a. Message number R300055Z May, your headquarters, subject as above.

    b. Letter, your headquarters, subject as above, dated 9 June 1972, with inclosure 1, listing camp site/village purification problems.

2. Major village problems confronting this command are as follows:

    a. Identification of trouble making U.S. personnel by ROK authorities and civilians.

    b. Racial discrimination.

    c. Narcotics and drug control.

    d. Prevention and treatment of venereal disease.

    e. Village environmental improvements.

    f. Range and training area encroachment.

3. There is an encouraging trend of improvement in only two problem areas:

    a. The first concerns the identification of rabble rousing U.S. service personnel by ROK civilians and officials. In May several such persons were identified by ROK officials; and unit commanders were able to take prompt disciplinary action against offenders.

    b. The second area of improvement is the elimination of racial discrimination in clubs and shops.

219

EAIDCS   26 June 1972
SUBJECT: Korean/American Friendship (KAFC) Meeting

(1) On 15 April U.S. and local ROK officials agreed that by 15 May
nine business establishments in North Tongduchon would relocate from in-
terior alleys to the MSR where they could be better controlled in this
regard and military police could better monitor them and provide patrons
more security. By 15 May seven of the nine establishments had relocated
to the MSR. One shop had closed, and the other moved to Tokko-ri.

(2) This action, and the placing of polarized clubs off limits,
improved racial relations by forcing integration. Success, however, is
due entirely to policy efforts.

4. Sale of narcotics and control of drugs continues as a major problem
which is a result of the inability, ineffectiveness, and apparent general
indifference to the problem by the Korean authorities.

a. It is relatively simple to prosecute on-post drug offenders.
However, off-post villages and dwellings are safe havens for drug ushers
and pushers, as well as militant racial groups. No substantial progress
will be made unless Korean authorities take meaningful action to eliminate
the sale of drugs and marijuana in the villages.

b. Since 21 February 1972 Korean National Police have arrested an
increased number of U.S. servicemen using marijuana or drugs. Only two
persons were in possession of dangerous drugs, while the others were
arrested on marijuana charges. However, unit commanders have not been
able to prosecute all cases. When U.S. servicemen are released to U.S.
authorities, the KNP's retain the evidence, i.e., drugs and/or marijuana,
presumably for prosecution in civilian courts under the provisions of
SOFA. In all marijuana cases ROK authorities waived jurisdiction,
apparently because of the minor nature of such cases and the anticipated
excessive costs to prosecute them.

(1) US authorities prosecuted only 50 percent of the marijuana cases
released to the U.S. because continuity in the chain of custody of the
evidence could not be proven. Prosecution is further complicated, or
becomes impossible, because of excessive elapse of time since the KNP
arrest and when the individual can be tried. This is due to the 15 day
waiting period (SOFA) wherein Korean authorities retain jurisdiction; and
the additional delay of complicated administrative procedures to obtain
the evidence for trial from the Korean prosecutor.

(2) To achieve more success in this area a recommendation should be
made to ROK officials that in all marijuana arrests the evidence (i.e.,
suspected/actual marijuana) be given to U.S. authorities with the appre-
hended individuals are released.

220

(3) In addition, ROK authorities should be encouraged to increase
the size of their police force in the camp villages—particularly their
detective and narcotics divisions, and to make more narcotics raids and
arrests to keep pressure on drug offenders and pushers.

5. Some U.S. civilians (generally former servicemen) living in camp site
villages have been identified as drug pushers. They are in Korea on
tourist visas, are not gainfully employed, and have no visible means of
support.

    a. If they are not gainfully employed, or do not have an income such
as retirement, ROK Government should deny them visas and expell them from
ROK.

    b. ROK embassies abroad should thoroughly screen applicants for
Korean visas, to identify and deny visas to such persons. Also, all ROK
consulates should be provided names of deported persons. This would prevent a U.S. citizen, once expelled, from obtaining a new visa from Japan
or another country close by.

6. **V.D. prevention and treatment.** There is an increase of over 50 percent in venereal disease cases. More alarming, there is an average of
30 cases of syphilis per month in the division.

    a. Local officials are seriously concerned about the increase in the
V.D. rate, and are doing their best to grapple with it. However, they do
not have enough facilities, staff, or equipment to gain the upper hand
in this growing struggle.

    (1) There is only one public health center in the city of Tongduchon,
vicinity of Camp Casey which has only 20 beds. Two patients occupy one
bed, a hallway of the building could be used during warm months for 10
additional bunks, or 20 more patients. Thus, the total patient capacity
would be 60.

    (2) Considering that the minimum stay for a gonorrhea case is 6 days,
the PHC could handle only 10 new cases daily. Treatment of 2,000 prostitutes in the Casey are would require 6.6 months.

    (3) The Public Health Center does not have sufficient or adequate
equipment to diagnose the various types of gonorrhea, or to detect
syphilis, and to prescribe required treatment in each case. It needs a
dark-field scope and equipment to make culture studies.

    b. ROK National Government should provide more support to assist
Tongduchon officials to combat venereal disease by providing a larger and
better equipped and staffed Public Health Center.

221

EA IDCS
SUBJECT: Korean/American Friendship (KAFC) Meeting

7. Sanitation of sightseeing establishments.

a. This is considered a ROK area of responsibility as it concerns the physical standards and appearance of civilian business establishments which cater to U.S. patrons.

b. The U.S. position on this point should be as outlined in USFK PD 1-3; inclosure one: any establishment that does not meet U.S. minimum standards, as outlined therein will be placed off-limits.

8. Counter-measure of society.

a. U.S. authorities do not have control over the management of ROK civilian business establishments.

b. There has been no change in U.S. policy regarding this subject. All U.S. patrons frequenting any establishment regardless of race, color, or creed will receive equal treatment and equal attention from management, employees and hostesses, or other persons frequenting the establishment for the purpose of deriving revenue from the patrons. Any business (or social) establishment which cannot provide this type of unbiased service must, in accordance with USFK PD 1-3, inclosure 1, be placed off-limits to U.S. personnel.

c. Proper guidance of abandoned women.

(1) This problem area is a by-product of an existing social situation, and perforce considered primarily a ROK area of responsibility.

(2) The two items of counteraction listed as American policy should be discarded. As they stand, they seem meaningless.

d. Removal of misunderstood view of Korea.

(1) KAMUP training has improved this situation.

(2) The ROK MND monthly tour for officers and senior non-commissioned officers should be extended to include a separate tour for selected lower enlisted grades.

(3) In addition, 2d Infantry Division has encouraged units to take advantage of Special Service Tours outside 2d Division area.

(4) Also there has been an increase in social and sports events among Korean Nationals and unit servicemen.

222

EAIDCS
SUBJECT: Korean/American Friendship (KAFC) Meeting

    d. <u>Control of civilian encroachment into firing ranges.</u>

    (1) "Offering of advance information training (3-4 days advance)" does not recognize the scope or magnitude of the problem. This is, to some degree, effective only during winter months when less training is conducted and armers cannot plant.

    (a) The greatest problem arises during the farming season. Farmers have not been restricted by local civilian authorities from planting on ranges. In some cases, as much as 95 percent of the range is illegally cultivated.

    (b) The U.S. military would have the legal right to conduct a mechanized field problem on the planted ground as long as it is within the boundaries of the land acquisitioned for a firing range. However, from political and moral points of view, the military commander is in a dilemma. Should he conduct an exercise on the planted land, or force the farmer to remove the undeveloped crops, or to abandon them, he then becomes the offender.

    (2) Recommend:

    (a) Local civilian officials and Korean National Police be compelled to prevent farmers from planting on ranges in the first place.

    (b) Where range land has been farmed:

    <u>1</u>. A monetary equivalent of the portion of land farmed be deducted from monies paid to owners of the land.

    <u>2</u>. Local officials and KNP's who did not prevent farming encroachment onto ranges be disciplined and removed.

    <u>3</u>. A permanent joint team at I Corps (ROK/US) Group be formed, responsible to I Corps Commanding General, to prevent range encroachment, to enforce exclusive acquisition rights, and to recommend corrective and/or punitive actions to the Commanding General, I Corps (ROK/US) Group, for violations.

10. Strengthening of ROK/US friendship ties. Comments, paragraph 9. c., above apply.

FOR THE COMMANDER:

                        PAUL P. ELLISON, JR
                        Colonel, GS
                        Chief of Staff

223

1. Health and Sanitation

    A. VD Control

        1) On 24 January 1972 Government instructed the following items
           for elimination or reduction of the causes of VD to the each
           provincial and city Government.

            a. All prostitutes in US Forces Camp Areas should be registered
               and examined of VD twice a week.

            b. All the infected VD patients should be treated with
               segregation.

            c. Health Center should provide monthly health education of
               VD prevention and necessity of its treatment for the
               prostitutes.

        2) Status of infected and treated patients by month 1972 is
           attached (Table 1, 2 .& 3)

    B. Sanitation

        1) On 22th March 1972 Government instructed the following items
           to the each provincial and city Government.

            a. Improvement of toilet-lavatory facilities in entertainment
               district.

                (1) To assure the adequacy of a running water supply in
                    toilets and lavatories.

                (2) To provide towel service, either paper or clean
                    cloth to customers utilizing lavatory facilities.

                (3) To provide service of washroom attendants whose duties
                    would include frequent cleaning

            b. Maintain of standardization of the facilities in Bars and
               the other establishment.

                (1) Workers in the facilities whould always carry their
                    Health Certificate.

                (2) A facilities which has not kept standardization with
                    regulation should be indicated to improve their
                    facilities within the term of validity.or punished
                    by regulation.

224

2. Narcotics and Drug Control

1) It was strengthened to control and check of narcotics and habitual drug especially in Dongduchon, Uijongboo, Bupyong, Pyungtaek and Paju by Korean Government.

2) The others excluded above mentioned areas was instructed to be made a thorouthgoing control by surveillance workers stationed in the respective areas.

3) Assignment of narcotics and habitual drug surveillance workers is attached (Table 4).

4) In collaboration with each district CID the surveillance workers carry out their activity.

5) The result of activities by month and by area is attached (Table 5 and 6).

225

Table 1

Status of Infection on VD by City and Province

City & Province	1971			1972 January			February			March			April		
	Reg. Pers.	Infect.	%	Reg.	Infect.	%	Reg.	Infect.	%	Reg.	Infect.	%	Reg.	Infect.	%
Total	244,938	33,259	13.6	17,656	2,957	16.7	16,937	2,767	16.3	19,461	3,053	15.7	20,797	3,060	11.3
Seoul	12,970	3,096	23.9	758	257	33.9	961	258	26.8	1,116	232	20.8	1,197	260	21.7
Pusan	51,094	5,963	11.7	2,642	484	18.3	2,102	282	13.4	3,227	485	15.0	3,218	456	14.2
Kyonggi	86,423	10,931	22.0	7,376	1,065	14.4	7,416	872	11.8	7,926	910	11.5	8,266	854	10.3
Kangwon	26,105	4,058	11.7	2,049	252	12.3	2,077	330	15.9	2,217	320	14.4	2,329	279	12.0
Choongpuk	1,010	27	2.6	60	0	-	63	0	-	71	0	-	75	0	-
Choongnam	10,967	1,547	14.1	639	101	14.6	682	117	17.2	623	125	20.1	621	107	17.2
Chunpuk	9,051	2,373	26.2	924	277	30.0	876	399	45.5	1,109	512	46.2	1,085	485	42.2
Chunnam	11,863	1,446	12.2	1,066	173	16.2	758	174	23.0	825	115	13.9	1,158	197	17.0
Kyongpuk	10,545	2,531	23.0	685	190	27.7	684	177	25.9	719	186	25.9	1,211	255	21.1
Kyongnam	21,117	1,980	9.4	1,176	140	11.9	1,107	131	11.8	1,404	142	10.1	1,441	177	12.3
Jaeju	3,793	307	8.1	227	18	7.9	211	27	12.8	224	26	11.6	196	17	8.7

Table 2

Status of Infection on VD by District in Kyonggi-Do

District	1971			January			February			March			April		
	Reg. pers.	Infect.	%	Reg.	Infect.	%	Reg.	Infect.	%	Reg.	Infect.	%	Reg.	Infect.	%
Total	68,842	7,307	10.6	6,482	759	11.7	6,655	513	8.9	7,051	645	9.1	7,268	525	7.2
Inchon	10,242	1,350	13.0	1,045	169	16.0	1,070	190	18.0	1,127	269	23.0	1,177	233	20.0
Yangju	17,540	1,600	9.0	1,877	308	15.0	1,894	220	12.0	2,200	167	8.0	2,229	127	5.0
Uijongbu	11,550	1,270	11.0	732	62	9.0	708	44	6.0	727	61	9.0	733	38	6.0
Pyungtaek	15,530	1,547	9.0	1,606	144	9.0	1,571	86	5.0	1,745	89	5.0	1,688	59	4.0
Paju	13,980	1,540	11.0	1,2222	76	6.0	1,412	53	4.0	1,252	59	5.0	1,441	68	5.0

1972

Table 3

Result of Examination of VD by Year (1961-1970)

Year	Total	Healthy	Status of Infection									
			Infect.	%	Syphilis	%	Gonorroea	%	Chncroid	%	Others	%
1961	139,104	107,901	31,203	22.4	1,273	4.0	26,761	87.0	1,450	4.0	1,719	5.0
1962	202,453	165,771	35,681	17.6	861	2.4	31,981	88.0	1,127	3.0	1,713	6.6
1963	294,461	249,503	44,958	15.3	1,471	2.2	40,634	91	935	2.0	1,917	4.8
1964	333,462	285,251	48,211	14.4	2,259	4	41,997	87.5	1,914	4	2,041	4.5
1965	328,829	283,106	45,723	13.9	3,230	6.5	37,366	80.4	1,647	3.5	3,489	9.6
1966	389,199	330,735	58,464	15.0	5,696	9.7	41,873	72	1,872	3	9,023	15.3
1967	342,068	293,712	48,256	14.1	4,596	9	34,275	70.8	990	4.2	8,495	16
1968	313,181	264,157	49,024	15.6	4,689	9.4	33,064	67.3	860	3.3	10,411	20
1969	286,375	237,014	49,361	17.2	3,625	7.3	26,003	53	1,149	2.7	18,584	37
1970	256,324	215,242	41,082	16	2,698	6.3	22,659	55	725	2.1	15,000	36.6

228

Table 4

Assignment of narcotics and habitual drug surveillance workers

Prosecutor's Off.	Ministry of Health & Social Affairs	City and Province	Total
Seoul	4 persons	Seoul city 2	6
Uijongboo	4	3	7
Inchun	2	1	3
Suwon	2	1	3
Taejeon	4	1	5
Chonju	2	2	4
Taegu	2	1	3
Pusan	5	1	6
Total	25	12	27

229

Table 5

Results of Narcotics and Habitual Drug Control
in US Force Camp Area by Month (1972)

Month	Total		Narcotics						Habitual Drug					
	No.of Cases	No.of related persons	Total		Over sale		Addict		Total		Over sale		Addict	
			Cases	Relat. pers.	Cases	Relat. pers.	Cases	Relate pers.	Cases	Relat. pers.	Cases	Relat. pers.	Cases	Relat. pers.
Total	85	113	29	36	26	33	3	3	56	77	51	66	5	11
Jan	6	10							6	10	4	7	2	3
Feb	10	13	4	5	4	5			6	8	6	8		
Mar	26	38	7	8	6	7	1	1	19	30	18	24	1	6
Apr	26	30	6	7	5	6	1	1	20	23	19	22	1	1
May	17	22	12	16	11	15	1	1	5	6	4	5	1	1

* In May : One smuggling case
(one person related)

<u>Results of Narcotics and Habitual Drug Control
in US Forces Camp Area classified by District (Jan '72-May'72)</u>

Table 6

District	Total		Narcotic						Habitual Drug					
	No. of Cases	No. of related persons	Total		Over sale		Addict		Total		Over sale		Addict	
			Case	Per.	Case	Per.	Case	Per.	Case	Per.	Case	Per.	Case	Per.
Total	85	113	29	36	26	33	3	3	56	77	51	66	5	11
Yongsan	8	12							8	12	6	9	2	3
Pusan	10	13	7	7	5	5	2	2	3	6	3	6		
Choonchun	3	3							3	3	2	2	1	1
Inchon	3	4	2	3	1	2	1	1	1	1	1	1		
Bupyung	6	8	5	7	5	7			1	1	1	1		
Soowon	2	2							2	2	2	2		
Uijeongbu	7	10							7	10	7	10		
Dongduchun	11	12							11	12	10	11	1	1
Pyungtaek	5	5							5	5	5	5		
Ohsan	5	5	1	1	1	1			4	4	4	4		
Paju	4	5							4	5	4	5		
Pochun	1	1	1	1	1	1								
Kunsan	1	1							1	1	1	1		
Taegu	19	32	13	17	13	17			6	15	5	9	1	6

* In Yongsan: One case of
smuggling (one per. related)

221

OFFICE OF THE PROVOST MARSHAL
4TH USA MISSILE COMMAND
V.D. STATISTICS

	RAINBOW	FLAMINGO	VICTORY	TWENTY-ONE	SKYLARK	METRO	STREETGIRL	OTHER	TOTAL
OCTOBER '71	1	2	1	3	1	1	7	3	19
NOVEMBER '71	3	0	5	1	2	2	7	1	21
DECEMBER '71	3	0	5	0	0	3	3	0	14
JANUARY '72	9	1	10	0	2	0	11	0	33
FEBRUARY '72	4	3	5	6	0	0	5	7	30
MARCH '72	6	0	5	3	0	0	11	7	32
APRIL '72	5	0	9	1	3	0	6	7	31
TOTAL	31	6	40	14	8	6	50	25	180
% FOR '72	19%	3%	23%	8%	4%	N/A	26%	17%	100%

Cleanup Drive Successful At U.S. Camp Villages

By Suh In-gyo

UIJONGBU — In less than two months after a special campaign was set off to clean up the surroundings of U.S. military camps throughout the country, a subdued but cheerful atmosphere has begun to prevail in this small city just north of Seoul.

Early this year President Park Chung-hee handed down an instruction to do away with various chronic ills rampant around camp towns where U.S. military personnel are stationed.

Since then joint efforts have been made painstakingly by customs, police, health, tax, and prosecution authorities in close cooperation with the U.S. military authorities to put an end to drug addiction, prostitutions, VD, smuggling, and violence in camp villages.

In the Uijongbu area a special committee for that purpose was set up early in January this year with membership of related organs to make the city better place to live in.

Led by Prosecutor Pak Jong-hi, the committee members meet regularly with the commander of a U.S. Army unit stationed in the area and work out more effective methods to bring this ambitious plan to success.

The results have already begun to turn up with the support of Korean residents and U.S. military personnel. Kim U-dong, chief of the Uijongbu customs office, said, "Recently we have had much less trouble to deal with. I am afraid we'll soon have nothing to do here."

He said his office handled 245 smuggling cases last year, amounting to up to 31,150,000 won, but he expected the number would be much less this year.

As a member of the special clean-up committee, the customs officials are only concerned with smuggling of foreign-made goods from U.S. military camps.

Each of five government organs has its own peculiar assignment in the camp town purification campaign. Police control contraband goods dealings. Health centers are for narcotics, and the tax office checks foreign-made liquors. The prosecution is the commander of the campaign. When military supplies are involved, they are dealt with by military investigators.

Uijongbu customs officials said that there were usually three typical types of smuggling. For example, goods are illegally brought out through the APO and PX under disguised legality, first in collaboration between Koreans and GIs, second through GIs' Korean girl-friends, and third by GIs commissioned by Korean middlemen.

It is said that a middleman gives a GI 5,000 won as a commission for buying a camera.

The campaign to clean up the surroundings of U.S. military camps originated from President Park Chung-hee's instruction after the U.S. military authorities repeatedly complained of drug addiction, VD, and violence rampant in camp villages. At that time it was known that about 70 percent of American soldiers suffered from VD.

The government is known to be planning various projects which will cost a lot of money to provide U.S. servicemen in Korea with the best surroundings with modern conveniences, but it cannot be the final solution to chronic maladies plaguing the camp towns, some thoughtful people believe.

The success of the current nationwide campaign largely depends on mutual cooperation between the government and the U.S. military authorities who will benefit from it.

Korean National Police - US Military Police C... ...ration and Coordination

Panel No. 2

Recommendations on which Implementing
Action has been Effected

Joint US-ROK Police Patrols be established where
US police authorities patrol off the military
installation.

...ter has been sent to all local area
...ost Marshal offices requesting an
...ase, or the establishment of joint
...ost US MP-KNP patrols.

Improved KNP-US Military Police cooperation and
coordination.

... letter referenced above stressed the
... to improve cooperation and coordination
...een US and ROK police agencies.

274

STATUS REPORT ON THE IMPLEMENTATION OF
SUBCOMMITTEE RECOMMENDATIONS

Panel No. 1

Recommendations on which Implementing
Action has been Effected

Local Community and Governmental Relations

Redesignation of CRAC to Korean-American
Friendship Councils and provide official
recognition of these Councils.

Official recognition of the redesignation of
CRAC to Korean-American Friendship Councils
(KAFC) was provided USFK units through the
Civil Military Affairs Newsletter (12-71). EA
Reg 550-5, Foreign Countries and Nationals -
Korean American Friendship Councils (awaiting
publication) reflects this change in designation.
This redesignation was also reflected in revised
USFK Policy Directive 5-3, dated 13 Jan 72,
which provides policy for the establishment,
composition, functions, reporting requirements,
and disestablishment of such Councils.

Panel No. 3

Recommendations on which Implementing
Action has been Effected

Elimination or reduction of the causes of VD through:
requiring VD carriers to undergo necessary treatment and instituting or intensifying cooperative
programs instructing personnel in causes, effects,
and elimination of VD.

Improved sanitation in toilet-lavatory facilities
in Korean clubs and establishments patronized by
US servicemen.

Barring of KN and minors from tax-free establishments catering to US servicemen.

Improve health and sanitation standards in eating-
drinking establishments catering to US servicemen.

276

Health and Sanitation

Results are intangible, due partly to inadequate
control and medical inspection facilities. The
ROKG has announced plans to open 16 additional
VD clinics in the camp-community areas and
will add approximately 100 doctors and nurses
to the counter-VD program. VD inspections
are being monitored more closely by ROKG
agencies. Infected entertainers are to be re-
strained and, if necessary, confined for treatment.
Korean Tourist Association affiliated bars and
other entertainment establishments have been
warned to more closely moitor entertainer-
clientels; if customer complaints indicate infected entertainers patronize bars, off-limits
action may result.

Significant upgrading has been noticed in all
camptown areas. Korean club owners have
increased the frequency of toilet-lavatory
cleanups and, in many instances, have installed
or improved running water supply in washrooms.

Korean National Police and the Health Ministry
(Women and Children's Section) are cooperating
in barring minors and unauthorized persons
from entertainment establishments.

See 2, above.

Panel No. 4

Recommendations on which Implementing
Action has been Effected

● Sets forth US-ROK responsibilities regarding
controls over sale and access to narcotics and
drugs in the ROK.

Familiarization programs be conducted jointly by
US-ROK law enforcement agencies to improve joint
operations.

No pharmaceutical sales of dangerous drugs to USFK
personnel without a prescription.

USFK prevent illegal flow of drugs into Korea via
US military post office channels.

●

Controls be tightened over habitual users of narcotics
and dangerous drugs, including action by US military
authorities to identify, segregate, treat and/or evacuate personnel identified as habitual users and by ROK
authorities to prevent special entertainers from continuing their business activities if habitual drug users.

Narcotics and Drug Control

Mutual agreement has been attained on the respective responsibilities of both parties.

Implementing efforts are currently being pursued
between military law-enforcement agencies and
the US Embassy as part of an overall program.

ROK officials currently are developing implementing measures to cope with sale of dangerous
drugs without prescription.

Increased surveilance by US postal personnel
and employment of newly installed X-ray
machines functioning on a fluoresence principal,
which produces an immediate image f package
contents resulting in detection of contraband,
including drugs.

US military, through urine testing, other medical
procedures, and apprehension, identify, segregate,
treat and/or evacuate personnel to the United
States who are identified as users. Treatment
continued until a cure is effected, including
outpatient treatment.

2개

Appropriate action against traffickers and experimental users be taken.

Appropriate action currently is being taken against these categories of offenders on a case-by-case basis.

278

Panel No. 5

Recommendations on which Implementing
Action has been Effected

● Improve measures for recovery of stolen US
Government vehicles and to check illegal
disposition of vehicles imported into the ROK
duty-free.

Provide information to ROK of disciplinary or
punitive actions taken against US personnel
who sell items to ROK nationals.

US-ROK authorities develop an additional list
of PX Commissary control items and better
monitoring procedures.

●

Larceny and Black Marketing

Joint policing efforts by US-ROK law-enforcement
agencies has already resulted in the recovery of
several stolen US Government vehicles.

A system for reporting such information is
established.

The US-ROK Joint Committee has assigned this
matter to its Finance (Personnel Affairs) Subcommittee for implementation. That Subcommittee currently is conducting joint negotiations
on this subject.

239

Panel No. 6   Race Relations and Equality of Treatment

Elimination of alleged discrimination against
black US servicemen in Korean clubs and other
establishments.

Elimination of alleged discrimination by Korean
hostesses in clubs catering to US servicemen.

Elimination of discrimination in the selecting
and playing of various types of music in clubs
catering to US servicemen.

Provide bilingual personnel for joint US-ROK
police patrols to improve communications
between US-ROK police personnel.

Korean clubs and businesses catering to US
personnel should be required to avoid names which
are offensive to the Korean public or imply racial
discrimination or exclusiveness.

Considerable progress has been attained, through
jointly coordinated ROK and US efforts, in eliminating this type of Discrimination.

Same as above.

Although improvements have been effected, some
complaints continue to be received regarding
types of music played, especially in the Camp
Humphreys Anjong-ni area.

US MPs in joint patrols contain an increasing
number of personnel with some degree of fluency
in the Korean language.

Through joint ROK-US efforts and coordination,
a high degree of progress has been achieved in
eliminating offensive name of establishments.

240

Panel No. 7   People to People Projects

Recommendations on which Implementing
Action has been Effected
_____

Encourage Korean organizations to conduct more
programs to enable US servicemen to visit Korean
homes and to get to know Korea and its people
better.

Recognition of importance of, and furthering support of "Hello Korea" program to bring it to more
US servicemen.

Increase availability of Korean-American cultural
material for use by both the Korean people and US
servicemen to enable Koreans and Americans to
increase their knowledge and understanding of each
other.

Recognition and support of People-to-People clubs in
Korea, organized under the People-to-People
International.

Nature of Implementing Action
_____

The home-visit program has been initiated in
several areas on a small scale. Strong efforts
is being given to the "Get to Know Korea" tour
and similar programs and it is planned to
increase the frequency of such tours.

Greater publicity is being given this program
through the Information Officers' Bulletin. The
Ministry of Culture and Public Information
(MCPI) has acquired an approved budget to
conduct two programs monthly.

MCPI has recently printed a large variety of
introductory publications in English on Korea,
large quantities of which have been made available to US servicemen. USFK is donating
various publications without cost to Korean
activities, agencies, and institutes.

Encouragement has been given to USFK units to
recognize and support the formation of additional
local clubs of People-to-People, Korea National
Headquarters, through publicity in the Civil-
Military Affairs Newsletter. USFK officials
have accompanied Korea National Headquarters
personnel in visits to US installation commanders
and ROK minicipal and local officials.

Encourage Korean students and US servicemen to take part in joint meetings, trips, and recreational programs, and maximize support of such programs by Korean social and professional organizations.

USFK personnel have attended charter ceremonies of new People-to-People Korean student clubs at several Korean schools to encourage joint US-ROK participation in activities sponsored by these newly chartered clubs. Joint Korean-American student meetings are conducted weekly at the Retreat Center. Advisors have been furnished by the USFK Public Affairs Office to seventeen English speaking student and youth clubs and some logistical support has been afforded these organizations.

242

공　　　　란

공   란

공 란

공   란

공   란

공   란

공   란

공 란

공　　　란

공　　　란

공   란

공   란

공   란

7. 제 12차.

1972. 7. 31.

256

外國軍基地周邊淨化綜合對策

72. 7. 20. 接受.

257

目　次

FY 73-74-75 3개年計劃

health. Sanitation
Racial Problems < street lighting
           back-alley club

- 1 -

258

推 進 経 緯

71. 12. 22   大統領 閣下께서 韓美1軍団 視察後 基地村 周辺浄化

對策을 樹立하도록 指示.

71. 12. 27   第1次 関係官 会議

12. 31   外国軍 基地村 浄化對策 委員会 構成

12. 31   該当部処 및 各市 . 道에 浄化對策 樹立 指示

72. 1. 28   第2次 関係官 会議

3. 17   中央對策 委員会 開催

4. 3   観光 休養센타 建立을 爲한 関係官 会議

5. 2   基地周辺 写眞 撮影 指示

6. 17   内務部 所管 事業計劃 最終 確定

259

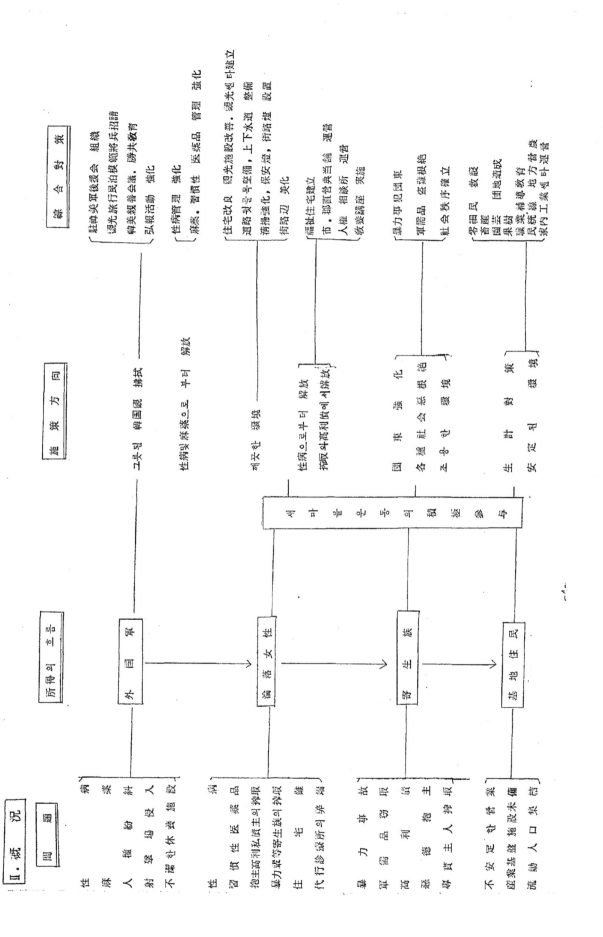

Ⅲ. 基 本 目 標

1. 조용한 環境造成 → 社会對策

2. 性病및 麻藥根絶 → 保健對策

3. 깨끗한 環境造成 → 環境淨化對策

4. 韓國觀 改善 → 親善活動對策

5. 安定된 環境造成 → 生活基盤造成對策

-5-

261

Ⅳ. 推進方向

1. 汎国家的으로 불붙고 있는 새마을運動精神을 基地村에 불어넣기 爲하여 淪落女性, 觀光業所 從事者, 住民等을 對象으로 하는 敎育을 強化하며 이러한 敎育強化를 通하여 이들의 自發的 參与를 促求한다.

2. 基地 周辺의 軍·官·民은 새마을運動精神에 立脚, 自体的으로 實踐이 可能한것은 優先 實施한다.

3. 問題解決에 있어서 軍·醫·行政機関 相互間의 協調関係改善에 努力하며

4. 各集団의 自治会를 組織, 이를 育成, 活用한다.

-6-

262

V. 綜合対策

（社会對策）

1. 射擊場 및 訓練場에 民間人 出入을 統制하여 訓練에 支障이 없도록 한다.

가. 軍警 合同으로 出入을 一切 統制한다.

나. 隣近 住民 182世帯(1,720名)에 對하여는 3個月間 <u>就勞 救護를 実施</u>, 生計에 支障이 없도록 하며 3個月後 転業토록 啓導한다.

   I日I人 3.6 kg(保社部 既存豫算) 66 %

다. 国防部는 京畿道 連川地域 射擊場 周緯 <u>31,640 坪을 追加 徴發</u>, 訓練에 支障이 없도록 한다 (既措置, 年內査定豫定)

라. 該当 市·郡은 自治会를 組織, 育成活用하며 軍은 <u>弾皮, 破片 等을 射擊終了後 自治会를 通하여 隣近住民에게 分配</u>하여 訓練에 支障이 없고 住民生計에도 도움을 주도록 한다.

2. 暴力事犯一掃等 社会秩序를 確立한다.

가. 合同巡察強化 (治) 130名 增員 (既措置)

나. 檢問所增設 (治) 19個所 (6個 常設, 13個 移動 檢問所) (11個로 修正, 既措置)

다. 団束車輛支援 (治) 11台 1,550萬원 (自体転用) 싸이카 41台 措置

라. 檢察支庁 運営 強化 (檢) 議政府, 水原, 仁川, 330萬원 (既措置)

-7-

263

마. 支派出所運營强化(治) 33 個所(実施中)

3. 軍需品 盜難을 防止하고 暗市場을 根絶시킨다.

　韓美合同 및 関係機関 協調로 団束을 더욱 强化한다.

　(内務部, 法務部, 国防部 및 関税庁)

　가. 人力增員 (関) 73名 1,819萬원 自体豫算 転用 既 措置

　나. 団束車輛支援(〃) 13台 986萬원 ⎤ 478萬원 自体豫算転用
　　　　　　　　　　　　　　　　　　　　⎰ 申請中
　다. 情報蒐集(〃) 891萬원 ⎦ 1,399萬원 既存豫算

　라. 5部合同 軍需品 団束(国) 222萬원(既存豫算, 実施中)

4. 惡德抱主와 高利私債로 부터 이들을 救濟하고 保證한다.

　淪落女性을 惡德抱主 高利私債業者의 搾取와 圧迫으로부터 解放
시키고 住宅難을 緩和하여 自立 更生할 수 있는 터전을 만드
는 한편 그들을 善導하고 権益을 保護토록 措置한다.

　가. 市. 郡直営 典当舖運営(楊州, 平沢)

　　　豫算 및 條例未備로 73計劃에 包含運営 豫定

　나. 人権 相談所 運営

　　　서울, 釜山, 仁川, 議政府, 水原, 大田, 群山 및 大邱等 8個所
檢察支庁 檢査로 하여금 人権相談을 担当토록 한다.

　다. 効奨講座 実施

　　　淪落女性들에게 効奨講座를 実施하여 그들의 教養과 資質을
높이는 한편 観光要員의 一員으로서의 矜持와 自負心을 갖도록 한다.

　　　年4回 定期 및 随時実施(11個地域) 170萬원

　　　(保社部, 市道 및 該当部에서 定期的으로 実施中)

264

5. 人種紛糾의 對策

觀光業所 從事者들에게 定期的인 敎育을 実施하여 音楽 等에
人偽的인 差別을 하지 못하도록 하며 違反業所에 對해서는 強
力히 行政 措置한다.

① 觀光業所 從事者 敎育 年4回 実施 (市. 道費, 実施中)

② 談話文 印刷 配付 1,350枚 54萬원 (〃)

265

（ 保健對策 ）

1. 外国軍과 淪落女性을 性病으로부터 解放시킨다.

　　豫算 2億 2千원中 1億 2千원은 自体豫算 転用 1億원은 糧穀으로

　　確保하여 内務部와 財源代替（ 自助勤労事業用糧穀 既 確保 ）

　가. 性病 診療所 完備

　　　代行 性病 診療所를 官営診療所로 転換하고 診療를 強化한다.

　　　（ 各種弊端是正 ）

　　　① 診療所 新築 및 補修 16棟 8,200萬원

　　　② 診療装備 補強 6組 1,072萬원（ 顕微鏡 스라이드 ）

　나. 検診治療 強化

　　　検診：70萬名 700萬원（ 8,800名 × 44週 × 2回 ）

　　　治療：26萬名 5,290萬원

　다. 医師, 看護員 等 要員確保 101名, 3,860萬원

　　　（ 医師 23, 看護員 23, 技士 23, 事務員 其他 23 ）

　라. 治療對象人員 給食賃 支援 2,830萬원

　　　（ 26萬名 1人 1日 107원 ）

2. 麻薬 및 習慣性 医薬品의 団束을 強化한다.

　　内務, 法務, 国防, 保社 및 関税庁 等 関係 機関의 団束 徹底

　　로 麻薬 및 習慣性 医薬品을 根絶하고 美軍側과 協調하여

　　APO（ 美軍事 郵便 ）를 通한 搬入 루트를 封鎖한다.

266

가. 韓美合同団束(保)　200件　620萬원(既存豫算, 実施中)

나. 団束車輛支援(〃)　　3台　620萬원(自体　豫算　転用)

다. 監視員　配置(〃)　　　　670萬원(既　措置)

라. 鑑識器具補強(〃)　100種　200萬원(自体豫算転用)

마. 鑑識太確保　및　管理(関)　6頭　194萬원(豫算確保)

267

（環境浄化対策）

　基地周辺의　住宅，道路，뒷골목，上下水道，街路辺，　観光業所施設等
을　整備，美化하여　<u>깨끗한　環境을　造成</u>한다.

※該当道，市，郡은　새마을　運動과　聯関하여　이미，自体的으로　実
施하고　있으며　京畿道의　境遇　4,30．現在　別紙와　같은　実績
을　올렸읍니다.

1.　　住　宅　改　良　　　　　953　棟　　　3,049　萬원（実施中）

　　가.板子．草家改良　　　　150　〃　　　　400　　〃

　　나.不良住宅撤去　　　　　348　〃　　　1,273　　〃

　　다.　　〃　改良　　　　　333　〃　　　1,068　　〃

　　라.便所改良　　　　　　　43　〃　　　　40　　〃

　　마.福祉施設　　　　　　　79個所　　　　268　　〃

2.　　道　　　路　　　　　　　　　　24,225　萬원　（　〃　）

　　가.道路拡張및整備　L=2,800m　　　　13,407　　〃
　　　　　　　　　　　　B=4〜35m

　　나.街路築造　　　　L=4,2km　　　　　5,190　　〃
　　　　　　　　　　　　B=4〜10m

　　다.카드레일設置　　L=1,4km　　　　　280　　〃

　　라.뒷골목舗装　　　L=5,1km　　　　　1,254　　〃
　　　　　　　　　　　　B=4〜9m

-12-

268

마. 側溝 設 置   L=4.2 km 2,610 萬원

바. 橋 梁 架 設   2 個所   160   〃

사. 步 道 舖 裝 (부력)   L=2.6 km
                        B=2~9 m 1,324 〃

3. 上 下 水 道   11,160 萬원   (実施中)
   가. 上 水 道   3 個所   4,600   〃
   나. 下 水 道   10 km   6,560   〃

4. 街路燈 및 保安燈   2,781 萬원   (地方費)
   가. 街 路 燈   567 燈   2,063   〃   (実施中)
   나. 保 安 燈   1.146 〃   718   〃   (〃)

5. 観光業所 施設을 改善한다.
   가. 不良施設改善   96 個所   5,360 萬원 (自担・実
                                            施中)
   나. 衛 生 検 査   月 1回
   다. 従業員教育   年 4回
   라. 観光休養센타   1 個所   5,651 〃(自担・既実施)

✓ 6. 観光센타建立
   追後 観光担当 秘書室과 協議하여 京畿道 平沢 및 東豆川
   地域에 綜合観光 센타 建立에 対한 最善의 結論을 얻도록
   하겠읍니다.

-13-

269

環境浄化実績　（京畿道）

72.4.30 現在

事　業　名	計　劃	実　績	備　考
不 良 住 宅 改 良	194 棟	182 棟	
울 타 리　改 良	26 〃	26 〃	
便 所 設 置	72 個所	67 個所	
花 壇 設 置	11 〃	9 〃	
案 内 板 設 置	3 〃	3 〃	
下 水 溝	48 〃	107 〃	
		(6.678 m)	
마 을 안 길 拡 張	3.696 m	4.626 m	
石 築 및 暗 渠	1.399 m	3.884 m	
小 橋 梁	14 個所	10 個所	
마 을 会 舘 建 立	4 棟	4 棟	
公 衆 沐 浴 湯	1 棟	2 棟	
小 河 川 改 補 修	1.100 m	2.100 m	
街 路 樹 （造 林)	500 本	560 本	
共 同 井 戸	22 個所	20 個所	
문 패 달 기	409 個	364 個	
道 路 補 修	210 m	210 m	

-14-

270

（親善活動対策 ）　　　　　　　　　　　　　　　　　　1

1. 駐韓美軍　後援会　組織　（中央）

　　海外弘報協会　主管下에　駐韓美軍　後援会를　組織、外国軍
　　将兵을　招請，観光旅行，民泊，姉妹結縁等　韓美間의　親
　　善을　図謀　한다。

　가．模範将兵　招請　및　旅行案内　（870　名）
　　　1泊2日　코-스로　古宮　및　市内와　産業施設　観光
　　　国防部　30名　（国軍의날）　90萬원（既確保 10. 1 実施豫定）
　　　文公部　480名　（月1回　40名）1160萬원　（42名　既実施）
　　　交通部　360名　（月1回30～40名）317萬원　（豫算確保）
　　　（国際観光公社）

　나．民泊周旋
　　　海外弘報協会는　駐韓美軍　後援会를　通하여　韓国家庭生活을
　　　経験함으로서　韓国에　関한　理解를　높이고、親善을　増進
　　　시키도록　民泊을　周旋한다。

　다．姉妹結縁
　　　海外弘報協会主管으로　各級　社会団体　및　学校에　依頼　姉
　　　妹結縁周旋。

2. 韓美親善　会議　組織　（地方）

　　　　　　　　　　　　　　　-15-

2기1

各地域　単位로　市長，　郡守主管　韓美親善会議를　組織하여　보다
많은　모임을　通하여　韓美間의　友宜를 敦篤히　하는　한편　韓
美間에　発生하는　諸般問提를　解決하고　懇談会，体育 大会等을
開催하여　親善을　図謀한다.

3. 勝共教育実施（ 1,500 名 ）

오늘날　韓国이　処하여　있는　軍事　및　非軍事的　実情.　特히
北傀의　排発危脅을　正確히　把握할　수　있는　機会를　賦与한다.

中央情報部　600 名 334 萬원（ 3 月부터　実施. 204 名既実施 ）
国　防　部　900 名 964　〃（自体豫算転用. 既確保　193 名
　　　　　　　　　　　　　　　　　　　　　既実施 ）

勝共教育（中情. 国防部 ）後　古宮. 워커힐等　市内観光　및　輸出
工団視察.

4. 各種弘報活動強化

外国軍에　対한　各種　弘報活動을　強化하여　韓国에　対한　올바른
印象을　浮刻시킨다.

가. 海外弘報 資料　刊行物　配付（ 文公部 ）10.200 部　（ 実施中 ）
나. 道. 市. 郡　弘報資料　刊行物　配付　　　　　　（ 〃 ）
다. 映画上映（ 文公部 ）地域文化院活用　　　　　（ 〃 ）
라. AFKN　時間　割愛

-16-

212

마. Hello Korea 푸로그램 (韓国綜合紹介行事)

　 年 36 回　 374 萬원　(5 回旣実施)

　　(映画 , 古典舞용 , 胎拳道 , 패얼 디스커 슌 , 刊行物配布)

바. Korea House 運営　(文公部)　(週 4 回)　(実施中)

사. 古宮無料観覧　(文公部)　　　　　　　(〃)

-17-

2ﾉ3

（生活基盤造成対策）

1 . 零細民救護

京畿道 一円 基地 周辺 零細民에 対하여 救護糧穀을 支給한다.

14,942 名　　523 M/T　　2,594 萬원（既存予算）

2 . 主産団地造成

各種団地（畜産，園芸，彩蔬，果樹）를 造成하여 基地 景気에 限

定되어 있는 所得源을 넓힌다.

計　2,113 萬원中，農林部　補助 815萬원　既確保

（1,200 萬원　融資　133 萬원　地方費，184 萬원　自担）

가 . 養　　　豚　　300頭　（農）765 萬원（自体予算転用申請中）

나 . 韓　　牛　　100″（″）800″（既措置）

　　　　　　　　　　　　　（融資）

다 . 菜　　蔬　　5ha（″）38″（″）

라 . 비닐하우스　122個所（″）198″（″）

마 . 果樹団地　　21ha（″）312″（″）

　　　　　　　　　　　　（181 萬원은融資）

3 . 職業輔導施設　拡充

職業輔導施設을 拡充하고 教育을 強化하여 職業의 機会를 賦与

한다.

가 . 職業輔導施設拡充　4個所（労）1,510 萬원（自体予算転用）

나 . 職業輔導実施　1,067 名（労）2,593 萬원（自体予算転用）

　　（理容，美容，編物，洋裁，手芸，自動車，打字）

-18-

274

다 . 韓美協同　職業　訓練　300 名(京畿道　美軍)

　　60 萬원 (講師料)

4 . 家内工業쎈타　設置

　　2 個所(勞)　　500 萬원　　(旣存予算 , 旣措置)

　　1 個所　新築　300 ″
　(　　　　　　　　　　　　　　)
　　1 個所　增築　200 ″

-19-

2115

VI. 総事業費 内訳

1. 対策別, 地域別 事業費 内訳
(単位:千원)

事業名	事業費	서울	釜山	京 小計	仁川	議政府	楊州	平沢	抜州	其他	忠南	全北	慶 小計	大邱	北 漆谷	其他
総 計	1,070,167	159,075	39,550	457,556	57,339	95,138	88,675	145,772	97,470	9,144	21,497	112,233	250,606	205,925	46,483	30,688
社 会 対 策	77,691	16,147	6,581	33,741	7,805	6,268	5,221	6,651	5,173	2,623	4,996	4,593	9,419	5,486	3,933	2,220
保 健 対 策	380,435	43,250	24,559	242,461	39,994	35,845	54,766	73,365	40,491	—	10,552	17,111	42,522	31,647	10,875	—
環境浄化対策	480,972	96,250	6,960	99,858	1,950	11,190	19,808	53,390	9,826	3,900	4,410	84,494	189,000	162,000	27,000	—
親善活動対策	33,358	1,000	450	2,050	320	320	320	520	570	—	270	270	850	550	300	28,468
生活善盤造成対策	97,711	2,428	—	79,426	7,270	7,515	8,558	11,846	41,616	2,621	1,275	5,765	8,817	4,242	4,575	—

-20-

2 . 国費財源内訳

部処別　予算別	合　計	既　存	目間転用	追加支援
総　　　　計	394,277	61,507	215,991	116,779
内務部地方局	101,035		－	101,035（地方交付税）
〃　治安局	24,074	3,900	20,174	
法　務　部	3,340		3,340	
国　防　部	12,760	2,220	10,540	
農　林　部	8,150	－	8,150	
商　工　部	3,000	－	3,000	
保　社　部	160,141	46,777	113,364	
交　通　部	3,172	－	3,172	
文　公　部	11,410	8,610	2,800	
関　税　庁	38,722	－	22,978	15,744（予備費，既措置）
労　動　庁	25,127	－	25,127	
中　　　情	3,346	－	3,346	

-21-

ᄅᄁᄁ

3. 地方費 및 自担財源内訳

予算別 / 市.道別	地　方　費			自　担
	計	市・道	市・郡	
総　　　計	524,915	396,195	128,720	150,975
서　　울	133,012	133,012		5,600
釜　　山	25,636	25,636		760
京畿 小　計	133,895	61,123	72,772	57,593
仁　川	25,803	7,055	18,748	6,500
議政府	19,972	6,894	13,078	4,500
楊　州	29,160	14,324	14,836	13,018
平　沢	36,221	21,225	14,996	8,000
坡　州	22,739	11,625	11,114	25,575
大　　德	5,219	2,716	2,503	1,110
沃　　溝	20,598	8,156	12,442	64,222
慶北 小　計	206,555	165,552	41,003	21,690
大　邱	174,470	149,554	24,916	16,690
漆　谷	32,085	15,998	16,087	5,000

-22-

278

Ⅶ．事後管理

1. 関係部処 및 該当道・市・郡은 中央対策委에서 確定된 事業에 対한 具体的인 事業計劃을 72．8．15限 青瓦台 政務秘書室에 報告한다.

2. 関係部処 및 該当 道・市・郡은 72.6. .부터 確定된 施策을 遡及実施한다.

3. 該当 道・市・郡은 毎月 10日까지 事業進度를 内務部長官에게 報告하여 中央各部処 및 内務部는 이를 青瓦台 政務秘書室에 報告한다.

4. 関係部処 및 該当 道・市・郡은 本浄化計劃을 発展시켜 基地 周辺 浄化를 為한 3個年計劃을 樹立 72．8．15까지 青瓦台 政務秘書室에 報告한다.

-23-

2٦9

공　　　란

공   란

공   란

공   란

공   란

공   란

공   란

공   란

공   란

공   란

공　　　　　란

공   란

공   란

공   란

공 란

공   란

8. 제 13차.

   1972. 9. 1

296

전(변)

내 무 부

관리 723 - $P615$ (70.2481)   1972.   8.   17

수신   회무부장관

참조   구미국장

제목   한미 합동 위원회 회의 개최 결과 조치

　　1. 미이 723 - 24403 (72. 8. 1)과 관련 있음.

　　2. 합동 위원회 회의록 (첨부물 제 25) 중 지방관서와 관련되는

사항을 별첨과 같이 해당되에 통보하였기 알려 드립니다.

첨부. 관리 723 - $P614$ (72. 8. 17) 공문사본 1부 끝

내   3Q050   무   부   장

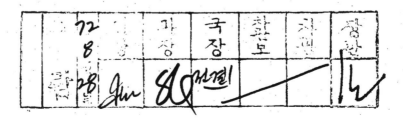

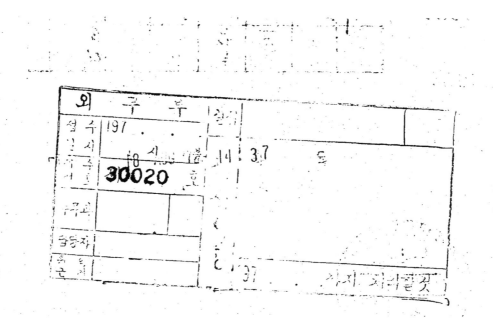

내 무 부

관리 723 -   (70.2481)   1972. 8. 17

수신   경상북도지사, 경상남도지사

참조   기획관리실장

제목   한미 합동 위원회 개척 결과 통보

한미 합동위원회 제175차 (72.7.6) 회의록중 귀도에 관련되는
사항을 아래와 같이 분체 통보하니 업무 수행에 참고할것.

1. 72. 6. 2 한미 합동 위원회 군민관계 분과위원 왜관소재
캠프 캐롤방문시 ······ "한국군서로 하여금 기지촌의 쓰레기를 적시
에 처리하면 가로등의 개수와 계천의 복개에 더큰 관심을 기울여 볼것"
(해당도 경상북도·관리 723 - 347. 72. 6. 17와 관련됨)

2. 72. 6. 9 군민관계분과위원 창원군 미제44 공병단을 방문
시 이 지역의 군민관계는 대체로 양호하나 성병감염율은 기지
촌의 업태부들의 대규모 이동이 있은 이후 과거 1, 2 개월전에 비하여
증가했다. 이 지역에 별문제점은 없으나 약품 통계를
보다 강하고 외근업무를 하는 한국 경찰의 배치가 요망됨" 끝

내 무 부 장 관

2981

공   란

공 란

산   림   청

보호 1153.42 -222/   1972. 8. 26.

수신 유엔군 사령부
      한미 합동 위원회 교체대표

제목 수렵면허 수수료 적용에 대한 건의

　　72.8.7자 귀하가 한미 방위조약에 의해서 한국에서 근무하는 미군부대
고용 미국인은 미국군인과 동등한 <u>수렵면허 수수료</u>를 적용해 줄것을 건의 한것은
충분히 이해가 되나 <u>조수보호 및 수렵에 관한 법률 시행규칙</u>에 국제연합군에만
특전을 부여하도록 규정되어 법규상 제한을 받는것으로서 귀의에 부응치 못하오니
이를 양지하시고 앞으로도 한국의 수렵행정을 위하여 많은 조언과 협조 있으시기
바라옵고 귀하의 건승을 빕니다.   끝.

산   림   청

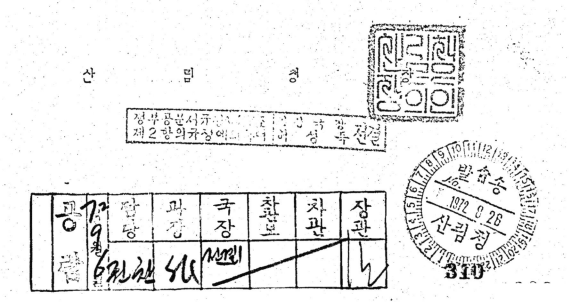

기 안 용 지

분류기호 문서번호	미이 723 -	(전화번호)	전 결 규 정 조 항 국장 전결사항
처 리 기 간			
시 행 일 자	1972. 8. 28.		
보 존 년 한			
보 조 기 관	과 장		
기 안 책 임 자	권 찬 북미 2과		
경 유 수 신 참 조	수신처 참조		
제 목	SOFA 합동위 제13차 군민관계 분과위원회의 개최 및 자료송부		

1. SOFA 합동위 군민관계 임시 분과위원회를 9. 1. (금) 14:00시 미측 SOFA 회의실에서 개최코저 하오니, 각 위원들은 필히 참석 하시기 바라며, 회의에 앞서 미측 초청으로 오찬회가 있음을 알려 드립니다.

2. 동 분과위원회 제12차 회의록을 별첨 송부하오니, 업무에 참고 하시기 바랍니다.

3. 지난 8. 18. 자로 김영섭 북미 2과장이 전임되고 그 후임으로 김기조 서기관이 임명됨에, 동 분위 한국측 대표가 경질되었으며, 간사에는 북미 2과 이승곤 외무서기관을 지명하였아오니, 양지 하시기 바랍니다.

첨부 : 제12차 회의록. 끝.

수신처 : 내무부장관 (지방국장, 치안국장)

공통서식 1-2(갑)
1967. 4. 4. 승인

190mm×268mm (1급인쇄 용지72g/m²)
조달청

302

311

법무부 장관 (법무 심장, 검찰국 장)

보 건사회부 장관, 문화공보부 장관, 교통부장관

청와대 정무수 석비서관 (내무.보 사담당 비서관)

주 미대사,

30쪽

JOINT COMMITTEE
UNDER
THE REPUBLIC OF KOREA AND THE UNITED STATES
STATUS OF FORCES AGREEMENT

August 22, 1972

Dear General Smith:

~~This is~~ to inform you that Mr. Kim, Kee-Joe
was ~~newly~~ appointed Chief of the North America
~~Second Section,~~ Ministry of Foreign Affairs ~~on~~
August 18, 1972 and assumed the post of Secretary
of the Joint Committee as well as Chairman of
the ROK component of the Ad Hoc Subcommittee
on Civil-Military Relations in replacement of
Mr. Kim Young Sup.

It is also advised that Mr. Lee, Seung-Gon,
was designated Secretary of the Ad Hoc Subcommittee
on Civil-Military Relations in replacement of
Mr. Kim, Kee-Joe.

Sincerely yours,

Kim Dong-Whie
Republic of Korea
Representative
ROK-US Joint Committee

Robert N. Smith,
United States
Representative
ROK-US Joint Committee.

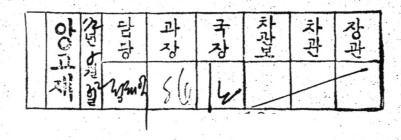

August 22, 1972

Dear General Smith:

I wish to inform you that Mr. Kim, Kee-Joe
was appointed as of August 18, 1972 to Chief of
the North America Section II, Ministry of Foreign
Affairs and concurrently assumed the post of
Secretary of the Joint Committee as well as
Chairman of the ROK component of the Ad Hoc
Subcommittee on Civil-Military Relations in
replacement of Mr. Kim Young Sup.

It is also advised that Mr. Lee, Seung-Gon,
Senior Staff, North America Section II, was
designated Secretary of the Ad Hoc Subcommittee
on Civil-Military Relations in replacement of
Mr. Kim, Kee-Joe.

Sincerely yours,

Kim Dong-Whie
Republic of Korea
Representative
ROK-US Joint Committee

Lt. Gen. Robert N. Smith, USAF
United States Representative
ROK-US Joint Committee

Agenda Item I

   I wish to thank you for your hearty welcome
to my first attendance as the new Chairman of
the ROK component of the Ad Hoc Subcommittee.

   It is a great pleasure for me to lead the
ROK members of the Ad Hoc Subcommittee and I am
sure I will do the very best I know how in
solving all the difficult tasks facing us today.

   I earnestly hope you cooperate with me
through thick and thin in this meeting.

                    Thank you.

306

Agenda Item II

I welcome the opportunity to introduce our
new secretary and two new members of this Ad Hoc
Subcommittee.

First of all, Mr. Lee Seung-Gon, new
Secretary of this Ad Hoc Subcommittee, a Senior
Staff of North America Section II, Ministry of
Foreign Affairs, is newly designated Secretary
of the ROK component of this Ad Hoc Subcommittee.
I am sure that he will contribute as much as
his predecessor toward the effective operation
of this Subcommittee.

May I introduce Mr. Lee?

Mr. Park-Hee-Tae, the Prosecutor of Claims
Section, Ministry of Justice, is designated a
new member of the ROK component in replacement
of Prosecutor Mr. Chung Ku-Young.

May I introduce Mr. Park?

Mr. Kwon Chan, also a Staff member of North
American Section II, Ministry of Foreign Affairs,

is designated a new member of this Subcommittee.
Mr. Kwon has worked from the inception of this
Subcommittee, so that I think he will fully
benefit from his experience and will demonstrate
his best ability at this time.

I am certain that the participation of these
new members will give a great impetus to better
solution of great many tasks involving US personnel
and Korean nationals.

Now, may I introduce Mr. Kwon?

306

Agenda Item VI.

Capt. Romanick and distinguished members:

I am sorry to learn that Capt. Romanick,
the most able Chairman of the Ad Hoc Subcommittee
on Civil-Military Relations, is leaving the
Subcommittee and I sincerely appreciate him
for the great contribution he has made so far
for about a year in carrying out our mutual
tasks.

I wish to extend my best wishes for his
good health and happiness.

309

공   란

공 란

공   란

공   란

공   란

공   란

공   란

공 란

공 란

공   란

공　　　　란

공   란

공 란

공   란

공 란

공   란

공　　　란

공   란

공   란

공   란

공 란

공　　　　란

공 란

공   란

공   란

공   란

공   란

공　　　란

공 란

공　　　　란

공   란

공   란

공   란

공 란

공   란

공 란

공   란

공   란

공   란

공   란

공   란

공 란

공 란

공　　　　란

공   란

공 란

공 란

공　　　　란

공 란

공   란

공   란

공   란

공　　　란

공   란

공   란

공 란

공　　　란

9. 제14차.

   1972. 9. 29.

367

기 안 용 지

분류기호 문서번호	미이 723 -	(전화번호)	전결규정 조항 국장 전결사항	
처리기간				
시행일자	72. 9. 25.			
보존년한			국 장	
보조 기관	과 장		협	
기안책임자	권 찬 북미2과			
경유 수신 참조	수신처 참조		통 제	
제 목	SOFA 제14차 군민관계분과위 회의개최 통보			

한.미 군대지위협정에 의한 SOFA 합동위 제14차 군민

관계 임시분과위원회를 72. 9. 29. 15:30 외무부 회의실에서 개최

키로 되었아오니 각 위원들은 필히 참석하여 주시기 바랍니다.

첨부 : 회의 의제 1부, 끝.	정서
수신처 : 내무부장관 (지방국장, 치안국장)	
법무부장관 (검찰국장)	관인
고통부장관	
보사부장관	
문학공보부장관	발송
청악대 정무수석비서관 (내무.보사담당비서관)	

공통서식1-2 (갑)
1967. 4. 4. 승인

190 mm × 268 mm (1 급인채 용지 70g ㎡)

조달청

TENTATIVE

AGENDA OF FOURTEENTH MEETING
AD HOC SUBCOMMITTEE ON CIVIL-MILITARY RELATIONS
1530 HOURS, 29 SEPTEMBER 1972, ROK CAPITOL BUILDING

I.   Presentation of Credentials by New US Chairman.

II.   Consideration of the Thirteenth Report of the Ad Hoc Subcommittee to the Joint Committee - ROK and US Presentations.

III.   Status Reports on the Implementation of Subcommittee Recommendations - ROK and US Presentations.

IV.   Plans for Future Ad Hoc Subcommittee Trips - US and ROK Presentations.

V.   Proposed Time for the Fifteenth Ad Hoc Subcommittee Meeting. 1530 Hours, Friday, 3 November 1972, in the US SOFA Conference Room.

VI.   Adjourn.

369

공 란

공   란

공   란

공   란

공   란

공 란

26 September 1972

Dear Mr. Kim:

This is to inform you that Captain Wallace E. Sharp, United States Navy, Assistant Chief of Staff, J5, US Forces, Korea, has been appointed to serve as Chairman of the US component of the Ad Hoc Subcommittee on Civil-Military Relations which was established by the ROK-US Joint Committee on 2 September 1971.

As you know, Captain Sharp has replaced Captain F. M. Romanick, and he will serve as Chairman of the United States component at the fourteenth Ad Hoc Subcommittee meeting scheduled for 29 September 1972.

Sincerely,

ROBERT N. SMITH
Lieutenant General
United States Air Force
United States Representative

Mr. KIM Dong Whie
Republic of Korea
Representative

10. 제 15차

1972. 12. 8

377

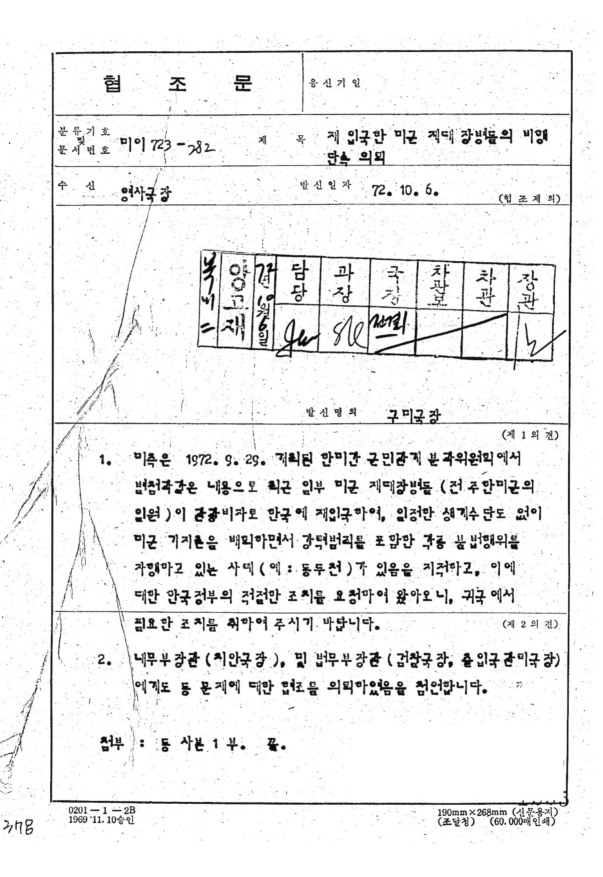

<table>
<tr><td colspan="2">협 조 문</td><td>응신기일</td></tr>
</table>

분류기호 및 문서번호	미이 723-282	제 목	재 입국한 미군 제대 장병들의 비행 단속 의뢰
수 신	영사국장	발신일자	72. 10. 6.　(협조제의)

북비	응고재	결재일	담당	과장	국장	차관보	차관	장관

발신명의　구미국장

(제 1 의 견)

1. 미측은 1972. 9. 29. 개최된 한미간 군민관계 분과위원회에서 별첨과 같은 내용으로 희군 일부 미군 제대장병들 (전 주한미군의 일원) 이 군용비자로 한국에 재입국하여, 일정한 생계수단도 없이 미군 기지촌을 배회하면서 강력범죄를 포함한 각종 불법행위를 자행하고 있는 사데 (예 : 동두천) 가 있음을 지적하고, 이에 대한 한국정부의 적절한 조치를 요청하여 왔아오니, 귀국 에서 필요한 조치를 취하여 주시기 바랍니다.

(제 2 의 견)

2. 내무부장관 (치안국장), 및 법무부장관 (검찰국장, 출입국관리국장) 에게도 동 문제에 대한 협조를 의뢰하였음을 첨언합니다.

첨부 : 동 사본 1 부. 끝.

0201 — 1 — 2B
1969 '11. 10승인

190mm×268mm (신문용지)
(조달청)　(60,000매인쇄)

기 안 용 지

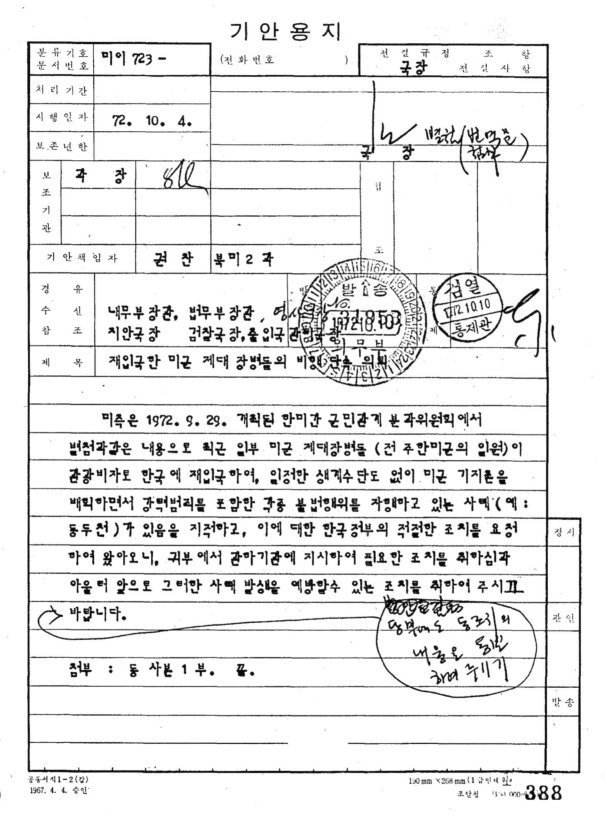

분류기호 문서번호	미이 723 -	(전화번호)	전 결 규 정 조 항 **국 장** 전 결 사 항
처 리 기 간			
시 행 일 자	**72. 10. 4.**		
보 존 년 한			
보 조 기 관	**과 장** *서명*		
기 안 책 임 자	**권 찬** **북미2과**		

경유수신참조 : 내무부장관, 법무부장관, *(외무부)*
치안국장, 검찰국장, 출입국관리과장, 의무부

제 목 : 재입국한 미군 제대 장병들의 비행 단속 의뢰

미측은 1972. 9. 29. 개최된 한미간 군민관계 분과위원회에서
별첨과 같은 내용으로 최근 일부 미군 제대장병들 (전 주한미군의 일원)이
관광비자로 한국에 재입국하여, 일정한 생계수단도 없이 미군 기지촌을
배회하면서 강력범죄를 포함한 각종 불법행위를 자행하고 있는 사태 (예:
동두천) 가 있음을 지적하고, 이에 대한 한국정부의 적절한 조치를 요청
하여 왔아오니, 귀부에서 관하기관에 지시하여 필요한 조치를 취하심과
아울러 앞으로 그러한 사태 발생을 예방할수 있는 조치를 취하여 주시기
바랍니다.

첨부 : 동 사본 1부. 끝.

공동서식1-2(갑)
1967. 4. 4. 승인   190 mm ×268 mm (1 급인쇄 원지)
조달청 (5 시) 000 m **388**

In its work to try to improve civil-military relations in the Korean camp communities, Ad Hoc Subcommittee personnel have found that there are many factors to be considered to deal with the situation which I would like to call to the attention of my Korean co-workers. It is a situation found in a few camp villages, especially Tongduchon. In that town a number of former American servicemen who had been discharged from the United States military forces, returned to Korea as civilians with Republic of Korea tourist visas. Some of these individuals live in the camp villages without visible means of support. One of these discharged servicemen who now is in Korea as a civilian is currently subject to trial in Republic of Korea court for implication in an alleged murder at Tongduchon. These American civilians who come to Korea on tourist visas are outside the jurisdiction of the United States military and while in Korea, they are under the jurisdiction of the Government of the Republic of Korea and subject to supervision by ROK governmental agencies and police.

480

We are calling attention of officials of the
Republic of Korea Government to this situation
since some of these individuals are sometimes
mistaken by Korean police as United States servicemen although they are actually in Korea under the
auspices of the Government of the Republic of
Korea rather than the United States Forces, Korea.
It is recognized that there are a large number of
former United States servicemen who have returned
to work in Korea with the United States armed
forces or legitimate businesses in Korea, and that
these lawabiding residents contribute to Korean-
American friendship and mutual understanding.
However, there are a few former American servicemen
who are a problem.

(FOR YOUR INFORMATION: The ROK officials
know of the existence of these individuals and
this low key approach is to endeavor to encourage
them to take appropriate action to deal with this
problem which is their responsibility, quietly
and effectively.)

781

3. In its work to try to improve civil-military relations in the Korean camp communities, Ad Hoc Subcommittee personnel have found that there are many factors to be considered to deal with the situation which I would like to call to the attention of my Korean co-workers. It is a situation found in a few camp villages, especially Tongduchon. In that town a number of former American servicemen who had been discharged from the United States military forces, returned to Korea as civilians with Republic of Korea tourist visas. Some of these individuals live in the camp villages without visible means of support. One of these discharged servicemen who now is in Korea as a civilian is currently subject to trial in Republic of Korea court for implication in an alleged murder at Tongduchon. These American civilians who come to Korea on tourist visas are outside the jurisdiction of the United States military and while in Korea, they are under the jurisdiction of the Government of the Republic of Korea and subject to supervision by ROK governmental agencies and police.

4. We are calling attention of officials of the Republic of Korea Government to this situation since some of these individuals are sometimes mistaken by Korean police as United States servicemen although

2

382

they are actually in Korea under the auspices of the Government of the Republic of Korea rather than the United States Forces, Korea. It is recognized that there are a large number of former United States servicemen who have returned to work in Korea with the United States armed forces or legitimate businesses in Korea, and that these law-abiding residents contribute to Korean-American friendship and mutual understanding. However, there are a few former American servicemen who are a problem.

(5. FOR YOUR INFORMATION: The ROK officials know of the existence of these individuals and this low key approach is to endeavor to encourage them to take appropriate action to deal with this problem which is their responsibility, quietly and effectively.)

3

내　　무　　부

외사　2068 - APCO　　　　　　　1972.　10.　16.

수신　외무부 장관

참조　구미국장

제목　재입국한 미군제대장병의 비행단속

　　1.　미이 723-31953 (72. 10. 6.) 과 관련임.

　　2.　본건에 관하여 당부에서는 외사 2068 -　　　　　(72.

10. 16.) 로 전국경찰에 지시, 기지촌 주변 비행 미군 제대장병에 대하

여는 강력히 단속토록 조치하였기 통보합니다.　　　끝.

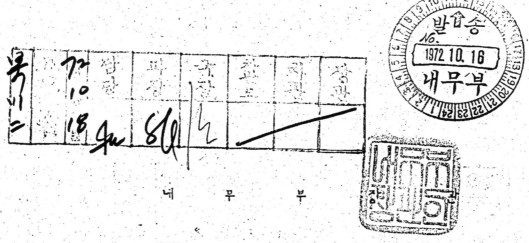

내　　무　　부

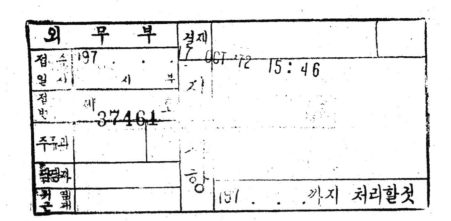

협 조 문	응신기일	

분류기호 및 문서번호	미이 723 - 300	제 목	재입국한 미군 제대장병들의 비행 단속 의뢰
수 신	영사국장	발신일자 1972. 11. 14.	(협조제의)

발신명의   구미국장

(제 1 의 견)

연 : 미이 723 - 282

연호 건에 관하여 법무부는 당부에 대하여 별첨과 같은
조치를 취하여 줄것을 요청하여 왔아오니, 귀국 에서 제대장병에
대한 사증 발급에 있어서 적절한 조치를 취하여 주시고, 그 결과를
당국에 통보하여 주시기 바랍니다.

(제 2 의 견)

첨부 : 법무부 공문사본 1 부.   끝.

외 무 부

정세보고처리전
(   )

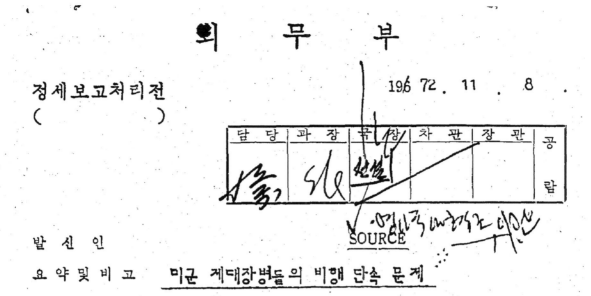

담 당	과 장	국 장	차 관	장 관	공 람

SOURCE

발 신 인

요 약 및 비 고   <u>미군 제대장병들의 비행 단속 문제</u>

1. 미군 제대장병들의 재입국 현황 파악은 불가능함.

   <u>이 유 :</u>

   1) 관광, 통과등의 명목으로 <u>48개월간 유효한 횟수사증</u>을 재외
      공관에서 쉽게 발급받아 수시로 출입국하고 있으며,

   2) <u>단기체류자 (2개월 미만)</u>들은 아무런 수속없이 국내에
      체류할수 있으며,

   3) 단기체류자중 거류신고를 해야하는 자 <u>(2개월 이상)</u> 라 할지라도
      거류신고시 제대장병의 신분 유무를 기재하는 제도가 없기
      때문 임.

2. 범법자 강제소한 문제

   1) 범법자에 대한 강제퇴거 조치는 법적으로 가능하나, 송환비용
      때문에 현실적으로 어려운 실정임. (72년도 총 예산 약 4천불)

   2) 고토 이들의 송환은 가급적 미군 군용기를 이용할수 있도록
      요청할 필요가 있으며, 미측으로 부터 미군인의 비행자와
      불명에 제대자들의 명단을 송부받아 한국 입국을 억제할
      필요가 있음.

786

법   무   부

검찰 821- **24354**   (70-2807)   1972. 11. 7.

수신 외무부장관

제목 재입국한 미군 제대장병들의 비행단속 의뢰

　　1. 미이 723-31953(72. 10. 6.)에 대하여 별첨과 같이 통보합니다.

　　첨부: 재입국한 미군 제대장병들의 비행단속 1부. 끝.

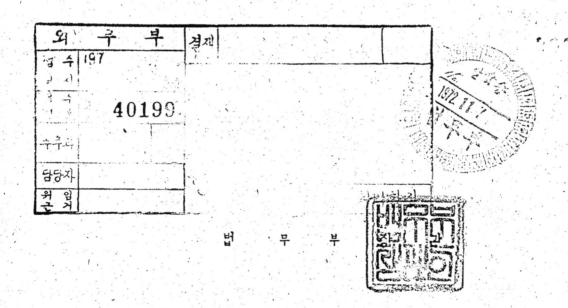

외 무 부	결재		
접수	197		
일시			
접수	**40199**		
번호			
처리과			
담당자			
위임 공람			

법   무   부

7 NOV '72 14:23

재입국한 미군 제대장병의 비행 단속

가. 미군 제대장병의 재입국 현황 및 명단에 대하여:

한, 미간 회수사증 발급 협정 (68. 3. 28)에 의거 미국인은 거주자격 (7-12)을 제외하고는 48개월간 유효한 회수사증(관광, 통과 및 체류사증)을 대한민국 재외공관에서 쉽게 발급 받고 사증발급일로부터 4년간 수시로 출입국할 수 있으며, 특히 60일 미만의 단기체류자(대기의 경우 관광사증 소지자) 등은 아무런 수속없이 국내에 자유로히 체류할 수 있고 거류신고를 하여야 하는 자(61일 이상 체류자)라 하드라도 신고시 현재의 신분관계 이외는 과거 제대장병의 신분유무를 기재하는 제도가 없어 확인 할 수 없음.

따라서 미군 제대장병의 재입국 현황 및 명단을 파악할 도리가 없음.

나. 범법자 또는 우범자에 대한 강제퇴거등 조치에 따르는 문제점에 대하여:

(1) 범법자에 대한 문제점

범법자중 일반형사범인 경우 금고 이상의 형을 받고 석방된자는 출입국관리법 제31조 8호 에 의거, 강제퇴거 조치를 할 수 있고 출입국관리법을 위반하거나 출입국관리법 제12조 각호에 연거한 입국금지 사유가 발생된 경우 강제퇴거 조치가 가능하며, 출입국관리사범은 경미한 사건을 제외하고는 대부분 강제퇴거의 대상(출입국관리법 제31조 각호)이 됨으로 대체적으로 범법자에 대한 강제퇴거 조치는 가능하나 송환비용이 문제임.

즉, 72년도 당부에 책정된 외국인 강제퇴거 예산이 총 1,621,000원(미화 약 4,000불)으로서 이것은 불과 미국인 10명만이 송환할 수 있는 비용(하와이 편도 379불)에 불과함으로 범법자의 수효가 증가할 경우 한정된 예산으로는 국비송환이 어려운 실정인바, 미군 당국과 협의하여 미군 제대 장병의 범법자에 대한 송환은 가급적 미군군용기를 이용할 수 있도록 협조가 요망됨.

388

2. 우범자에 대한 문제점

   우범자에 대한 강제퇴거조치는 출입국관리법 제12조 각호에 열거된 입국금지 사유에 해당하는 사실이 발생된 경우를 제외하고는 실제상 불가능함으로 이들에 대한 강제퇴거 조치는 어려운 점이 많은 바, 미군측과 협의하여 미군인으로 재직시 비행자와 불명예 제대자등 한국입국을 억체크저 하는 자의 명단을 수시 송부받아 이들에 대한 현지사증 발급을 제한함으로서 이들의 입국을 사전에 방지할 수 있음.

협 조 문　　응신기일

12.9.12ºº(?)

<table>
<tr><td>문서기호
및
문서번호</td><td>영사 725-239</td><td>제 목</td><td>재 입국한 미군 제대장병의 비행단속</td></tr>
</table>

수 신　구미국장　　발신일자 72. 12. 6　　(협조제의)

발신명의 영 사 국 장

(제 1 의 견)

대 : 미이 723 - 300

대호 요청에 의거 별첨 사본과 같이 조치 하였음을 회보 합니다.

첩부 : 영사 842 - 16001 문서 사본 1부.　끝.

(제 2 의 견)

<table>
<tr><td rowspan="2">북
비
고
감</td><td></td><td>담
당</td><td>과
장</td><td>국
장</td><td>차
관
보</td><td>차
관</td><td>장
관</td></tr>
<tr><td>12
9</td><td></td><td></td><td></td><td></td><td></td><td></td></tr>
</table>

0201-1-2B
1969. 11. 10승인

190mm×268mm 신문용지 50g/m²
조달청 (200.000매 인쇄)

790.

관 인 생 략

의　　　무　　　부

영사842-16001　　　　　　　　　　　　　　1972. 11. 25.

수신: 각 재외공관장

제목: 미군 제대 장병 (전주한 미국 군인)의 입국 허가 통제

　　　1. 한.미간 군민관계 분과 위원회 에서 미측은 별첨 사본과
같이 최근 일부 미군 제대 장병들(전 주한 미군의 일원)이 관광 비자로
한국에 재입국 하여 일정한 생계 수단도 없이 기지촌을 배회, 강력
범죄를 포함한 불법 행위를 자행하고 있는 사태가 있음을 지적하고 이에
대한 적절한 조치를 취하여 줄것을 아측에 요청 하였읍니다.

　　　2. 가, 미국인에 대한 사증 발급은 한.미간 휘수 사증 발급
협정(68.3.28.)에 의거 거주 자격(7-12)을 제외하고는 48 개월간 유효한
휘수 사증을 재외공관 에서 쉽게 발급 받고 4년간 수시 출입이 가능하며,
재입국 현황 및 명단도 파악이 불가능 하다는 점과,

　　　　나, 재외공관 에서 사증을 받고 입국한 미국인중 범법자는
형사범인 경우, 금고 이상의 형을 받고 석방된 자는 출입국 관리법 제31조
8호 및 12조 각호에 의거 강제 퇴거토록 되어 있으나, 송환 비용(예산)이
부족하다는 점 등의 이론가 있어 관계 법무부로서도 그 처리에 고충을
겪고 있는 실정에 있읍니다.

391

   3. 따라서 각 공관에서는 상기한 점등을 참작 하시어 미 제대 장병(전 주한 미군)의 사증 발급에 있어서는 신중을 기하여 주시고, 신언 등이 분확실 하거나 또는 유법자로 보이는 자들에게 데하여는 사증 발급 을 억제 하는 등 가능한 제반의 통제 조치를 취하여 주시기 바랍니다.

첨부: 사본 1부. 끝.

                        외   무   부   장   관

                 ┌─────────────────────┬──────────────┐
                 │ 정부 공문서 규정 제7조   │ 영 사 국 장   │
                 │ 제2항의 규정에 의하여   │ 기 진 홍   전 결 │
                 └─────────────────────┴──────────────┘

392

Report of Prosecutor Hyun Hong Joo, the Ministry of Justice, on the problem of certain former U.S. service-men in camp communities, at the 15th meeting of Ad Hoc Subcommittee on Civil-Military Relations held in the U.S. SOFA Conference Room on December 8, 1972.

On September 29 of this year at the 12th meeting of this Ad Hoc Subcommittee, the U.S. Chairman Captain Sharp called the attention of Republic of Korea government officials to the problem of former American servicemen who had been discharged from the U.S. Forces and subsequently returned to Korea as civilians with tourist visas. It has been noted that some of these people live in camp villages without visible means of support, and are suspected to be engaged in illegal activities in and around camp communities.

Recognizing troublesome nature of this problem and the R.O.K. government jurisdiction over these people, officials of the Ministry of Justice had a series of discussion to solve this problem, and in the course of the discussion, they found there are several factors which should be considered in their effort to straighten out situation.

1. According to the present procedure for granting visas and permitting entry to foreigners into Korea, whether it be under tourist visa or other kind of visa, it is very difficult for the Korean government to examine former occupation of the visa applicants, not to mention, detecting criminals or would-be criminals unless they are recorded in the list of undesirable persons.

2. Although a foreinger who found guilty of criminal offences can easily be ordered to be expelled from the country as has been evidenced by the recent example of a former U.S. serviceman who was found guilty of violation of the Habit-forming Drug Control Law, it is rather difficult under present practice to order an alien to be expelled against his will on mere suspicion of illegal activities.

3. Expenses for deportation or expulsion of foreigners are supposed to be met by R.O.K. government budget, and amount of fund available for this purpose is rather limited.

The R.O.K. officials feel that because of these shortcomings in present practice which cannot be easily changed without substantial increase in budget and substantial change of procedure which is bound by pertinent domestic legislations as well as international agreements and practices, it is very desirable for both the R.O.K. and the U.S. government to discuss following suggestions which will assist law enforcement in immigration area to a great degree.

They suggest:

1. That the U.S. authorities will provide the R.O.K. authorities the informations concerning prior criminal and / or disciplinary record of the persons who, in the judgement of the U.S. authorities, belong to above mentioned category of former U.S. servicemen and their presence in the R.O.K. is undesirable for both the R.O.K. and the U.S. ; and thereby enable the R.O.K. government to deport them on proper legal grounds or to refuse extention of visa.

394

2. That the U.S. authorities discuss among themselves, and tell the
   R.O.K. authorities the result thereof, the possibility of using
   the U.S. military transport means for deporting these problematic
   civilians.

   Meanwhile, the R.O.K. government will continuously follow up this
   problem, and ask pertinent U.S. authorities to help them in exerting
   their efforts in straightening out this situation which is troublesome
   for both governments.

395

기 안 용 지

분류기호 문서번호	미이 723 -	(전 화 번 호 　　　)	전 결 규 정 　 조 　 항	
			국장	전 결 사 항
처 리 기 간				
시 행 일 자	1972. 12. 6.		부 장	
보 존 년 한				

보 조 기 관	과 　 장	84		협		
				조		
기 안 책 임 자	권 　 찬	북미2과				

경 유			발		
수 신	수신처 참조			38456	
참 조			신	107212.	代 理

제 　 목	SOFA 　 제 15차 군민관계 분과위 회의개최 통보

　1.　　한.미 군대지위협정에 의한 SOFA 합동위 제 15차 군민

관계 임시분과위원회를 72. 12. 8. 15:30 미측 회의실에서 개최

키로 되었아오니, 각 위원들은 필히 참석하여 주시기 바랍니다.

　2.　　각 위원들은 관계부처가 집행중에 있는 기지촌 시책 현황의

진척도를 준비, 동 회의에서 보고하여 주시기 바랍니다.

　첨부 : 회의 의제 1 부. 끝.

수신처 :	내무부장관 (지방국장, 치안국장)	정서
	법무부장관 (검찰국장)	
	교통부장관	관인
	보사부장관	
	문화공보부장관	
	청와대 정무수석비서관 (내무.보사담당 비서관)	발송

1261

TENTATIVE

AGENDA OF FIFTEENTH MEETING
AD HOC SUBCOMMITTEE ON CIVIL-MILITARY RELATIONS
1530 HOURS, 8 DECEMBER 1972, US SOFA CONFERENCE ROOM

I.   Status Reports on the Implementation of Subcommittee Recommendations - ROK and US Presentations.

II. Report on Status of Present Program and Future Plans of the "Base Community Clean-Up Committee" - ROK Presentation.

III. Plans for Future Ad Hoc Subcommittee Trips - US and ROK Presentations.

IV. Proposed Time for the Sixteenth Ad Hoc Subcommittee Meeting, 1530 Hours, Friday, 12 January 1973, in the ROK Capitol Building.

V.   Adjourn.

1. 성병의 원인 제거
가. 성병 진료소
외국군 주둔지역에 성병관리를 철저히 실시하기 위하여
11개지역에 성병진료소를 72.12.30 까지 완공, 73년도
부터 진료를 실시할 계획임.
설치지역

구분	개소	지역
서울	1개소	이태원
부산	1	초량
경기	5	부평, 의정부, 양주, 평택, 파주
충남	1	대덕
전북	1	군산
경북	2	대구, 칠곡

나. 일제단속
기지촌주변에 성병의 전염원을 색출하기 위하여 일제
단속을 실시하고 있음.
1) 단속기간 : 72.10.29 - 12.31
2) 단속대상지역 : 외국군 기지주변 전역
3) 단속반 : (보건소요원, 관할경찰서, 부녀계직원) 합동반편성
4) 단속기간중 적발된 미등록자 및 검진불응자는 검진을
   실시하여 감염자로 판명된자는 전원 수용및 용원
   치료 시켰음.

398

12.5현재 실적

12.5현재 등록수 : 11,936명

12.5까지 검진수 누계 : 87,457명

" 감염수 누계 : 7,455명

(수용치료 : 2,147명 통원치료 : 5,308명)

다. 일제검진

외국군 기지주변에 대한 성병의 정확한 감염실태파악과

전염권을 제거할 목적으로 의과대학 부속병원 소속

전문요원의 협조를 얻어 일제검진을 실시하였음.

1) 실시지역 : 서울및 경기도(인천, 의정부, 양주, 파주, 평택)

2) 실시기간 : 72.12.27 ~ 12.6(10일간)

3) 검진대상 : 기지주변 특수여성 전원

4) 검진결과에 대한 검사는 국민보건연구원에서 실시

중에 있음.

5) 지역별 검진반

서울 (용산) 1개반

경기 (인천) 2

(의정부) 1

(양주) 3

(파주) 2

(평택) 3

계 12개반

399

2. 73년도 사업계획

가. 성병관리

사업명	계획	예산
성병관리		23,341,000
성병검진	1,240,000	지방비
성병치료	101,500	22,776,000
성병진료소운영	10개소	지방비
요원인건비	58명	"
행정요원	1명	565,000

400

5. 성병감염실태

시도별 성병 감염실태

	10월 누기			9월			10월		
	등록수	감염자	%	등록수	감염자	%	등록수	감염자	%
계	200,759	34,290	17.1	20,839	3,697	17.7	22,397	5,361	23.9
서울	11,196	2,625	23.4	1,135	268	23.6	1,362	416	30.5
부산	29,902	4,487	15.0	2,623	448	17.1	2,951	495	16.8
경기	82,101	12,661	15.4	8,713	1,598	18.3	8,872	2,682	30.2
강원	21,769	3,187	14.6	1,938	369	19.0	2,142	374	17.5
충북	598	7	1.2	62	2	3.2	63	5	7.9
충남	6,460	1,131	17.5				847	128	15.1
전북	10,212	4,386	42.9	1,032	387	37.5	978	397	40.6
전남	9,618	1,475	15.3	1,787	146	8.2	1,585	227	14.3
경북	10,970	2,635	24.0	1,380	319	23.1	1,415	397	28.1
경남	15,667	1,477	9.4	1,947	138	7.1	1,735	190	11.0
제주	2,296	219	9.5	222	22	9.9	447	50	11.2

지역별 성병감염실태(경기도)

	등록수	감염자	%	등록수	감염자	%	등록수	감염자	%
계	72,044	10,590	14.7	7,351	1,524	20.7	8,109	2,608	32.2
인천	11,112	2,621	23.6	931	264	28.3	1,039	255	24.5
의정부	7,185	609	8.5	729	109	14.9	755	82	10.9
양주	21,602	3,422	15.8	2,354	484	20.6	2,510	1,062	42.3
평택	17,959	2,284	12.7	1,888	370	19.5	2,029	776	38.2
파주	14,106	1,654	11.7	1,449	295	20.4	1,776	433	24.4

401

I. Eradication of Veneral Diseases Sources

1. Veneral Diseases Clinic

In order to make a through going control of
veneral diseases in the areas adjacent to foreign
military bases (camp communities), 11 V.D. clinics
will be constructed not later than the end of 1972
and will start the examination and treatment activities in 1973.

Constructed province	No. of clinics	Districts
Seoul	1	Itaewon
Pusan	1	Chryang
Kyonggido	5	Buppong *Uijeongbu* *Yangju, pyongtack . paju.*
Chungnam	1	Daedog
Chunpuk	1	Koonsan
Kyongpuk	2	Taekoo, Chilkok
Total	11	

2. General Control

A General Control is being implemented in all camp
communities for the purpose to find out the epi-
demic Sources of V.D.

A. Period   : 29 Oct. - 31 Dec. 1972

B. Object   : All base communities

C. Control team : Composed of health Center Personnel,
                   police and woman welfare personnel.

D. The un-registered persons, checked during the above
   period, and unexaminees are examined in force and
   confirmed cases will be treated in the clinics, ad-
   mitted or not.

402

Accomplishment as of 5 Dec. 1972

No. of register   :   11,936

No. of examinees   :   87,457

No. of infected cases : 7,454

(Inpatients : 2,147, out-patients: 5,308)

3. A mas-examination was made for the registered or checked
   cases with the cooperation of the experts in the refered
   medical school hospitals, for the purpose to get the
   exact information of V.D. infection and remove the infection sources.

   A. Area : Seoul and Kyonggido (Inchon, Euijongbu,
             Yangju, Paju, Pyongtaek)

   B. Period : 27 Nov - 6 Dec. (10 days)

   C. Object : All prostitutes in camp communities.

   D. The Examinned specimen are transpered to NIPH
      for confirmation.

   E. Examining team by districts

Seoul Yongsan		1 team
Kyonggi,	Inchon	2 team
	Euijongboo	1 "
	Yangju	3 "
	Pajoo	2 "
	Pyongtaek	3 "
	Total	12 team

403

II. 1973 V.D. Control Plan

Program	Target	Government Budget
V.D. Control	Total	23,341,000
Examination	1,240,000	Local budget
Treatment	101,500	22,736,000
Operation of V.D. clinics	10 clinics	Local budget
Wages & Subsidies for V.D. workers	58	- do -
Administrative personnel	1	565,000

464

Present Status of V.D. Infection by City and Province

	Total as of end of Oct.			September			October		
	Registered	Infected	%	Registered	Infected	%	Registered	Infected	%
Total	200,789	34,290	17.1	20,839	3,697	17.7	22,397	5,361	23.9
Seoul	11,196	2,625	23.4	1,135	268	23.6	1,362	416	30.5
Pusan	29,902	4,487	15.0	2,623	448	17.1	2,951	495	16.8
Kyonggido	82,101	12,661	15.4	8,713	1,598	18.3	8,872	2,682	30.2
Gangwondo	21,769	3,137	14.6	1,938	369	19.0	2,142	374	17.5
Chungbukdo	598	7	1.2	62	2	3.2	63	5	7.9
Chungnamdo	6,460	1,131	17.5				847	128	15.1
Chunbuk	10,212	4,386	42.9	1,032	387	37.5	978	397	40.6
Chunnam	9,618	1,475	15.3	1,787	146	8.2	1,535	227	14.3
Kyungbuk	10,970	2,635	24.0	1,380	319	23.1	1,415	397	28.1
Kyungnam	15,667	1,477	9.4	1,947	138	7.1	1,735	190	11.0
Jeju	2,296	219	9.5	222	22	9.9	447	50	11.2

Present Status of V.D. Infection by Districts

	Total as of end of Oct.			September			October		
	Registered	Infected	%	Registered	Infected	%	Registered	Infected	%
Total	72,044	10,590	14.7	7,351	1,524	20.7	8,109	2,608	32.2
Inchon	11,112	2,621	23.6	931	264	28.3	1,039	255	24.5
Euijongboo	7,185	609	8.5	729	109	14.9	755	82	10.9
Yangju	21,682	3,422	15.8	2,354	484	20.6	2,510	1,062	42.3
Pyungtaek	17,959	2,284	12.7	1,888	370	19.5	2,029	776	38.2
Paju	14,106	1,654	11.7	1,449	295	20.4	1,776	433	24.4

가. 마약 및 습관성 의약품 사범단속 (기지촌)

　　기지촌 정화대책의 일환으로 각종 유흥업소 (고고

클럽 등)와 기지촌 주변에서 외국인을 상대로 하는

마약 및 습관성의약품 사범을 근절하고자 각 지방

검찰청 및 지청에 마약감시원을 상주시켜 전담검사의

수사지휘에 의거 계속적인 단속에 임하는 한편 부정

기적으로 한·미합동 (각지구 C.I.D. 및 O.S.I.)

기동 단속은 물론 특히 계엄하 관계기관 (군·경)과

의 합동단속을 보다 강력히 실시하여 72, 11 월말

현재 351 건에 455 명을 적발 의법 조치 (외국인

73 명은 미관계기관에 이첩) 하였음.

나. 미군 병사에게 조제되어 유출되는 습관성 의약품

판매 통제문제

~ /~

407

습관성 의약품 관리법 제19조 판매제한 등의 규정은 있으나 동시행령 제5378호 습관성 의약품 품목 동 시행령 규칙 제21조 판매허용량의 범위에는 처방전이 없어도 판매할 수 있도록 되어 있으나,

1) 각 약업소에 대하여 어떠한 경우라도 미군에게는 처방전·없이는 습관성 의약품을 판매하지 않도록 1972. 7. 7 약1446-9396호로 행정지시를 취하했으며

2) 습관성 의약품인 Amphetamine 류는 현재 국내에서 수입 및 판매된바 없으며 Barbiturate 계통의 약물중 특히 Secobarbital은 습관성 의약품 관리법 발효후 수입 및 생산 판매된바 없고 기타 Barbiturate는 복합제제로서 사용되며 그외

~2~

408

Phenobarbital 이 단일 제제로서 시판된바 있으나

습관성 의약품 관리법에 의거 엄격히 통제되고 있

어 남오용의 우려가 없음

한미 합동 공동으로 습관성 의약품 단속을 위한

감시 업무를 강화하여 불미한 사례가 없도록 노력

하겠음.

사 업 실 적

월별	계	마 약			습 관 성 의 약 품		
		밀수	밀매	중독자	밀수	밀매	중독자
10	40 42		~~4~~ 5	5 5		23 24	8 8
11	159 199	1 5	14 37	4 6	1 1	76 85	63 65
누계	351 (64) 455 (73)	1 5	42 98	12(1) 14(1)	3 (3) 4 (4)	180 (18) 209 (19)	113 (42) 125 (49)

지 역 별

월별	계	서울	부산	경 기						경북	전북	충남
				소계	인천	의정부	양주	평택	파주			
10	40 42	 10	9 10	27 28	5 5	4 4	7 7	7 7	4 5		1 1	3 3
11	159 199	23 32	12 15	62 69	10 11	11 11	16 16	22 26	3 5	18 23	12 18	32 42
누계	351(64) 455(73)	50(8) 65(11)	30(1) 35(1)	174 208	30(1) 46(1)	34(12) 37(12)	45(13) 51(16)	51(8) 56(9)	14(3) 18(3)	47(17) 76(17)	15(1) 23(3)	35 45

※ ( )는 미군인 검거수임.

~4~

410

Law enforcement on Narcotics and Psychotropic
Substances Violation in the Vicinity of Foreign
Military bases.

a) The Ministry of Health and Social Affairs has dis-
patched narcotic Law Enforcement Officers to
every distric Prosecutor's offices and their
Branch offices and conducted Law enforcement
under the supervision of Public Prosecutor's
as well as keeping strong control with cooperation of joint R.O.K.U.S. agencies like every
local C.I.D. and O.S.I. and with appropriate
military and police agencies under the Martial
Law for the purpose of elimination of narcotics
and psychotropic substances, violation and disorders in the vicinity of foreign military bases
and special enter-tainers like go go clubs as a
means of government's clean up movement.
At the end of November, 1972, 351 cases in-cluding
455 persons were found guilty and taken legal pro-
ceedings. (73 foreign violators were transfered
to related organization).

b) Problems concerned with sales of psychotropic substances illegaly dispensed and issued from U.S.
Military Personnels.

Article 19 of Drug Abuse Control Law regulates the limitation of sales but in the limitation of permitted doses of Article 21 of minister's order No. 5378, it allows the sales of these drugs without physician's prescription. Ministry has ordered every retail pharmacy and drug selling store not to sell any psychotropic substances to any U.S. Military Personnels without physicians prescriptions on July 7, 1972.

Amphetamine-like substances a kind of Psychotropic Substances have not been imported and sold in Korea and government has not allowed dealers to import, produce and sell secobarbital among Barbiturate derivatives since taken effect of Drug Abuse Control Law and other barbiturates are available in the form of combination drugs. Only single preparation of Phenobartal is marketed and strictly controled by Law in no danger of being abused.

Government will take every possible measures in order to preclude any violance and disorders with respect to narcotics and psychotropic Substances with joint R.O.K. and U.S. operation.

Results of Activity

month \ class	Narcotics			Psychotropic substances		
	smuggle	illicit sale	addict	smuggle	illicit sale	addict
10		4	5		23	8
	1	5	5		24	8
11	1	14	4	1	76	63
	5	37	6	1	85	65
Total	1	42	12 (1)	3(3)	180(18)	113(42)
	5	98	14 (1)	4(4)	209(19)	125(49)

4/7

Geographical Activity

month	total	Seoul	Pusan	Kyunggi Do sub total	Inchon	Yechung-boo	Yangju	Pyeng Taek	Paju	Kyungbuk	Chun-buk	Choong-nam
10	40		9	27	5	4	7	7	4		1	3
	42		10	28	5	4	7	7	5		1	3
11	159	23	12	62	10	11	16	22	3	18	12	32
	199	32	15	69	11	11	16	26	5	23	18	42
Total	351(64)	50(8)	30(1)	174	30(1)	34(12)	45(13)	51(8)	14(3)	47(17)	15(1)	35
	455(73)	65(11)	35(1)	208(21)	46(1)	37(12)	51(16)	56(9)	18(3)	76(17)	23(3)	45

* ( ) is number of arrested U.S. Military Personnels.

題目: 麻藥및 習慣性醫藥品團束狀況

1. 團束 統計 (72. 1 ~ 11末)

　가. 檢擧人員
　　　美國人 : 60名 (1名拘束. 59名移牒)
　　　韓國人 : 640名 (422名拘束. 202名不拘束. 16名卽審)

　나. 押收品量
　　1) 麻藥 : 5,016g (韓國人)
　　2) 習慣性 : 大麻草粉末等 165,505g (韓國人및美國人)
　　　　　　　 L.S.D. 300錠 (美國人)
　　3) 罌粟 : 108,074本 (韓國人)

2. 團束活動
　가. 地域別 團束 責任制 實施
　나. 密輸루―트 및 製造元 把握 封鎖
　다. 情報網 確保 檢擧工作強化
　라. 廣犯地域에 對한 檢問檢索
　마. 處罰 强化

3. 協調關係
　麻藥및 習慣性醫藥品 事犯 團束은 어느나라
　든지. 國內問題에 局限되지 않고 國際的인問
　題로서. 國家相互間에 積極的인 協調로서
　團束을 强化해야 할것임

공 란

공   란

공 란

공   란

공 란

공 란

공 란

공   란

공 란

공   란

공   란

공　　　란

공   란

공　　　란

공　　　　란

공   란

공   란

외교문서 비밀해제: 주한미군지위협정(SOFA) 38

주한미군지위협정(SOFA) 군민관계 임시분과위원회 3

초판인쇄 2024년 03월 15일
초판발행 2024년 03월 15일

지은이 한국학술정보(주)
펴낸이 채종준
펴낸곳 한국학술정보(주)
주 소 경기도 파주시 회동길 230(문발동)
전 화 031-908-3181(대표)
팩 스 031-908-3189
홈페이지 http://ebook.kstudy.com
E-mail 출판사업부 publish@kstudy.com
등 록 제일산-115호(2000. 6. 19)

ISBN 979-11-7217-049-3 94340
     979-11-7217-011-0 94340 (set)